PRAYERS FOR
ALL PEOPLE

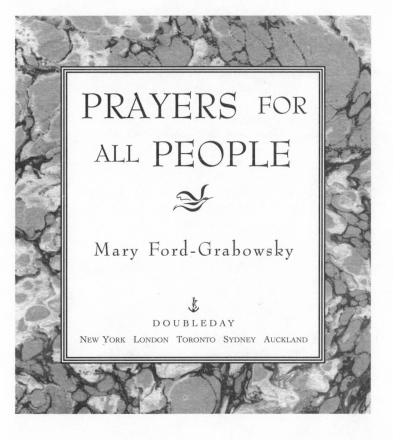

PRAYERS FOR
ALL PEOPLE

Mary Ford-Grabowsky

DOUBLEDAY

NEW YORK LONDON TORONTO SYDNEY AUCKLAND

To Axel and Tara

PUBLISHED BY DOUBLEDAY
a division of Bantam Doubleday Dell Publishing Group, Inc.
1540 Broadway, New York, New York 10036

DOUBLEDAY and the portrayal of an anchor with a dolphin are trademarks
of Doubleday, a division of Bantam Doubleday Dell Publishing Group, Inc.

Design by Julie Duquet

Library of Congress Cataloging-in-Publication Data
Ford-Grabowsky, Mary.
Prayers for all people / Mary Ford-Grabowsky.
p.   cm.
Includes index.
1. Prayers.   2. Life change events—Religious aspects.   I. Title.
BL560.F67   1995

291.4′3—dc20   95-7916
                                                                  CIP

ISBN 0-385-47643-4
Copyright © 1995 by Mary Ford-Grabowsky
All Rights Reserved
Printed in the United States of America

November 1995
1 3 5 7 9 10 8 6 4 2
FIRST EDITION

CONTENTS

❧

Special Acknowledgments

To Axel and Tara: there are no words vast enough to say what I would like to say to you. Thank you for all your help with this book; for the soaring Dartmouth spirit; for the love that never dies.

To the faculty, administration, and staff of Princeton Theological Seminary, for nurturing in me for seven years "the love of learning and the desire for God."

To Mr. William O. Harris of the Department of Archives and Special Collections, Princeton Theological Seminary, and to your staff, for your kind assistance with research.

To Ms. Kate Skrebutenas of Speer Library at Princeton Theological Seminary, for invaluable help with research.

To Ms. Denise Schwalb, for skillful assistance and grace under pressure.

To the Reverend Dr. Matthew Fox, for your translations of Meister Eckhart, for filling the world with *viriditas*, and for daring to "move the Western world."

To Acharya Palaniswami and Swaminatha—and to Satguru Sivaya and Subramuniyaswami—for the traditional Hindu Indian spirit of love that animates *Hinduism Today*, Himalayan Academy Publications, the book *Natchintanai*, and all the magnificent Hindu prayers from India that you sent me for this book. *Om Shanti Shanti Shanti*.

To Brother David Steindl-Rast, for the beautiful prayer you contributed to this book and for the spiritual beauty you bring to the world.

To Dr. Huston Smith, a very great scholar, for sanctifying marriage with the lovely prayer written for this book.

To Sri Eknath Easwaran, for a deeply moving prayer, and for the example of the totally self-giving life.

To Brother Wayne Teasdale, for the mystical prayer you wrote for this book, and for your great work on behalf of the cosmic community.

To Dr. Andrew Harvey, for your prophetic prayer, and for helping the West to recover its mystical soul.

To Mother Tessa Bielecki, for the "earthy joy" and sparkling vitality in the prayer you wrote for this book. To the Reverend William McNamara, OCD, descendant of John; to the Reverend Thomas Reynaud; and to everyone at the Spiritual Life Institute.

To Dr. Ronald Nakasone, for the spirit of gentle beauty in the meditation you wrote for this book.

To Ling Lucas and Ed Vesneske, Jr., of the Nine Muses and Apollo agency: to you, Ling, for the depths of spiritual feeling and insight you brought to this project; to you, Ed, for your peaceful presence and always patient counsel.

To Lori Lipsky, the Doubleday editor whose idea it was to celebrate the riches of the human lifecycle through a book of global prayers, my most heartfelt thanks. I have deeply loved the sacred task.

To Frances Jones of Doubleday, who loves beauty: thank you for guiding your brown pencil over this manuscript with so much skill and warmth.

To Frances Apt of Doubleday, a most gifted copy editor, who wished that this book would "do good in the world," very special thanks.

To Sister Lorette Piper, rscj, for the depths of compassion in your struggle for justice and in the powerful prayer you wrote for this book.

To the Reverend Robert Jones, for "Lauren," and for your great ability to see God in everyone and everything.

To the Reverend Dr. Eugene Blair, for your lovely prayers and for the example of spiritual courage you bring to ministry.

To Dr. Elizabeth Lopez, for your kindness in allowing me to reprint the prayers of Lisa Boscane.

To the Reverend Charles Cummings, OCSO, for the treasured gift of prayers, especially your own and your translation of Charles de Foucauld's.

To Swami Nityananda, for a prayer reflecting a deep experience of pain and love.

To the Reverend Dr. Marguerite Manning, for all your help with research and for all your love.

To Mrs. Anita Wheatcroft, for your loving prayer, poetry, and ministry.

To Dr. Mary-Theresa McCarthy, for the spirit of love in the

beautiful translations you wrote for this book and for your translations of Lisa Boscane's poetry.

To Mr. Thomas Feeney, for your great ability to translate the contemplative spirit in *A Christo Crucificado* and all the translations you wrote for this book.

To the Reverend Margaret Payne, for your creative and generous help in trying to find the source of two Lutheran prayers.

To Mr. Andrew Schelling, for the exquisite use of words in your translations of Mirabai, your books, and correspondence.

To Dr. Sulekh Jain, for assistance with research and for deepening my appreciation of the Jain religion, prayers, *sutras*, ethics, and philosophy.

To Dr. Irfan Ahmad Khan, a great sholar of Islam, for your exhaustive help with Islamic prayers and historical data.

To Mr. Robinton M. Rivetna, of the Federation of Zoroastrian Associations of North America, for so greatly aiding my research on Zoroastrian prayers.

To Ms. Eve Roshevsky, of Women of Reform Judaism in New York City, for your generous help in research on Jewish prayers.

To Dr. Adelgundis Führkötter, a consummate scholar at the Abtei Sankt Hildegard in Bingen, Germany, for assisting my research on Hildegard of Bingen.

To the Carmelite nuns of Indianapolis, for permission to reprint your prayer, "Waiting for a Child."

To Dr. Victor Laurie, for the sheer brilliance in your assistance, for the depths you bring to friendship.

To Mrs. Donna Laurie, a truly "enspirited" friend, for the caring, energy, and creativity you gave to this book.

To Mrs. Linda Lamb, of Princeton, New Jersey, for your superb photography, cherished friendship, and the utter delight of your presence in my life.

To Dr. George Lamb, for your suggestions for this book, for the gift of laughter, and the pleasure of your company throughout the years.

To the following people, my most heartfelt gratitude for all your assistance in research and for your prayers:

Dr. M. Amir Ali, Dr. Perle Besserman, Dr. Beatrice Bruteau, The Reverend Patrick Connor, Sr. Kathleen Cox, rscj, and the lower-school faculty and students of Stuart Country Day School in Princeton, New Jersey, Ms. Emily Sargent Councilman, Ms. Pamela Frankenfield, Dom Laurence Freeman, OSB, Rabbi Joseph Gelberman, Dr. Arthur Green, Ms. June Moreau, Pir Vilayat Inayat Khan, Mr. Herbert A. Kenny, Dr. Robert Muller, Ms. Janet Perlman, Mr. Charles Rampp, Ms. M. C. Richards, Swami Dayananda Saraswati, P. K. Swami, Dr. Manfred Steger, Dr. Arthur Stein, Dr. William M. Stephens, The Reverend Dr. Adrian van Kaam, Ms. Mariel Walters, Mr. Dann Ward, Ms. Priscilla White.

INTRODUCTION

Prayers for All People

The words of a beautiful Christian prayer from the Middle Ages sound quite different from a ninth-century Maya prayer or a Navajo prayer from the eighteenth century, but their spirit and power are identical. A prayer about death from the Celts in the British Isles over a thousand years ago consoles and comforts in the same way as a Hebrew Psalm from 1200 B.C.E.

Prayers are the same all over the world—in every religion and every century. Prayers spring from a universal human longing and need to know God and to understand mystery. In Thailand, Sri Lanka, or Belgium, as in the United States, prayers awaken spiritual beauty and inspire love. Hindus, Zoroastrians, and Jains, like Christians and Jews, have experienced since the beginnings of their ancient religions the power of prayer to transform and to heal and give hope. All genuine prayers from all spiritualities and faith traditions give to people who pray a sense of aliveness, of meaning and purpose, of playing an active role in the great Divine drama unfolding daily and hourly throughout the world.

We address the Divine with many names—Allah, Krishna,

Mbamba, Imana, the Tao, the Absolute—but there is only one Holy Presence, one Reality, whatever the language in which one prays: there is only one God beyond all the world's names for God. Lifting one's heart to the Divine in the depths of sorrow and in the heights of joy is a universal human act, everywhere the same and equally sacred—in Africa, China, the Middle East, and Central America.

In this sense, no prayer is unique—however ancient, however remote it may seem. Beliefs, ideas, doctrines underlying a topic may vary, but the human experience from which a prayer arises is the same, and the One God-Beyond-All-Our-Gods, the Holy One to whom we all pray, is the same. Each prayer in this book has an equivalent in each of the world's great religions. Three prayers for the newborn, for example — Pygmy, Bahá'í, and Presbyterian—express through very different styles the same special joy and pride and gratitude that parents and grandparents feel when a child is born. Because of the universality of our spiritual response to life's experience, the prayers in this book have been arranged to celebrate the sacredness of the human lifecycle, the sacredness of the lifespan of the individual and of all men and women—in Italy, Norway, Algeria, Argentina, any land in the world, in any century.

Only one prayer in this collection seems to be unparalleled in the spiritual literature of the world, an American classic called "A Sixteen-Year-Old Gangster's Prayer," which will convey to future generations the unique character and tragedy of 1990s' violence.

Prayers for All People contains some familiar prayers, some rarely seen in the West, and some never published before. The previously unpublished prayers come from disparate sources. A number were written specifically for this book by leading scholars and contemplatives, such as Professor Huston Smith, Brother David Steindl-Rast, Sri Eknath Easwaran, and Mother Tessa Bielecki. Others were specially translated for this book: "Behold Us, the Colombians," for example; "If Your Body Does Not Resemble Mine," from Lebanon; "Give Me Someone," from Japan; and several others. There are prayers that have been handed down for thousands of years — perhaps six thousand years — such as the Zoroastrian prayer for marriage, the Jain prayer for forgiveness, and the lovely Hindu prayer for coming-of-age.

Some of the most beautiful prayers in this collection are contemporary. Like Brother Wayne Teasdale's "Cosmic Prayer for the Sacred Community," written for this book in 1994, they come from the spiritual renaissance that is rapidly bursting into flame all over the world. Other prayers mark the beginning of the West's recovery of its mystical soul: Arthur Waskow's exquisite "Covenant of Consolation," for example, and Lisa Boscane's "After Climbing Mount Carmel." Like Andrew Harvey's magnificent "Prayer to the Divine Mother" — written only months ago and published here for the first time—these prayers show that the spirit of Rumi, Saint Francis, and Saint John of the Cross is swiftly returning to the West after four centuries of suppression. More and more, prayers are highlighting love, the sacred feminine, passion, eros, and ecstasy.

Out of the ashes of Western civilization as we knew it, and the ruins of the East, a new global spirituality is emerging for the twenty-first century. Based less on faith and belief than on personal and mystical experience of the soul and the Presence of God, this universal spirituality is presented and celebrated here in the sacred oneness of prayers by and for all people.

The Sacredness of the Lifecycle

Within the holy light that sweeps across the world, illumining all that is dark, warming all that is cold, the sacred cycle of time unfolds through the moon's great revolutions, the turning seasons and flowing tides, birds rushing south and returning north again. At the center of sacred time, the high purpose and meaning of all existence is both revealed and concealed, a miracle and a mystery.

There are no words deep enough to explain or convey the holiness of time eternally cycling and spiraling through the vast universe. Scriptures and the literature of wisdom hint at the truth; the Book of Ecclesiastes comes as close to the truth as writing can in its simple, sublime, and profoundly beautiful symbols and images:

> *For everything there is a season,*
>   *and a time for every matter under heaven:*
> *A time to be born, and a time to die;*
>   *A time to plant, and a time to reap;*
> *A time to kill, and a time to heal;*
>   *A time to break down, and a time to build up;*
> *A time to weep, and a time to laugh;*
>   *A time to mourn, and a time to dance (Ecclesiastes 3:1–5).*

Life's Passages

Within these unending cycles of change, of loss and new-ness that sacred time brings in its wake, the life of the individual passes in transformations, as Rilke said, that bring to an end forever something that was and create something entirely new. Unplanned, unexpected, unpredictable—for the Spirit works through surprises—these transition times, these trans-formative eras in the human lifecycle, weave the threads of personal experience from birth until death into a brightly colored pattern of completeness, fulfillment, individuality. As a Holy Day imprints the bleak circle of the year with mean-ing, so each of the great moments in the lifespan mark it indelibly with direction and Divinity.

Each transitional event in the course of a life is an arche-typal event and an intensely spiritual experience, imparting infinitely more power and possibility than humanity generally knows. The Divine undercurrent in all creation runs like a murmuring brook through each watershed experience, di-recting and guiding and drawing the lifecycle toward fruition, toward fulfillment in the future of the ultimate purpose in every atom and every cell.

Among all possible pivotal points in the lifespan, nine events stand out as the most crucial, most critical, as those with the most potential for personal growth, for self-knowledge, salvation, wholeness, personhood. These nine turning points include birth, coming of age in young adulthood, marriage to the companion of one's life, the quest for God, commitment to the way of prayer, the first encounter with life-threatening illness, unavoidable suffering, arriving at elderhood, the threshold from death to Eternal Life.

Deep within these nine primal events, God's radiant loving energy, which from all eternity moves the whole shimmering cosmos to expand and continue expanding, gently beckons the individual to expand — to grow, mature, develop, change, and become the full self one was meant to become. Each of life's threshold times, each watershed, liberates and illuminates more and more of the hidden inner self, setting free new abilities and gifts, enlarging even our capacity for growth. "Ages pass," observed Tagore, "and still Thou pourest, and still there is room to fill."

Life's passageways, often long and dark and narrow, unavoidably entail suffering. "The shell must be cracked," Meister Eckhart said, "if what is in it is to come out." Like a grain of wheat, the heart opens only by breaking, by shattering, and the process of sacred shattering begins with suffering as deep as the sea. But the crossing from childhood to young adulthood, from good health to poor health, from midlife to elderhood, any crossing, especially the nine this book describes, end in joy. With each transition, a person becomes, as

Paul Tillich wrote, a new creation, reborn through the pain of radical relinquishment to the fruitful, self-giving life.

Prayers for Life's Passages

All cultures throughout recorded time have celebrated life's great transition times religiously, through formal symbolic rituals ranging all the way from the loveliness of a Russian Orthodox wedding mass to the violence and savagery of human sacrifice. At the heart of all these religious rites of passage have arisen immeasurable, invaluable stores of living prayers, which are—and will always be—the world's most precious possession. These cherished prayers serve to recognize, bless, honor, love, and glorify the Divine origin and goal of all creation, and elevate each moment in the lifespan to the level of sacrament.

Prayers for life's passageways, like all authentic prayers, awaken and direct transformative energies that no other human resource or activity, not even art or music or love, can arouse. Prayer is the primary work of the spiritual life; the words of a prayer give life to the spirit, as Saint Paul said. Once prayer begins, images and aspirations well up in the soul like springs of water, and seeds sewn in eternity begin to sprout. And when the habit of prayer is firmly established in the heart, Divine light warms and illumines the soul, gently transforming self-centered striving into love.

Rilke described in a majestic and prayerful poem the holiness of his—and all humankind's—experience of life's passages:

> *I live my life in growing orbits*
> *which move out over the things of the world.*
> *Perhaps I can never achieve the last,*
> *but that will be my attempt.*
> *I am circling around God, around the ancient tower,*
> *and I have been circling for a thousand years.*

Prayers for All People celebrates the life of the individual as it curves out and carves silent circles in the invisible universe, drawing nearer with every passing year to "the ancient tower"; the Tao; the Blessed One.

BIRTH

"I have called you by name. You are mine . . . You are precious in my sight, and I love you" (Isaiah 43:1, 4). The Jewish scriptures teach that the creature made in the image and likeness of God, whose body and soul are made in the image and likeness of God, contains a spark of Divinity that yearns for nothing more than loving and being loved. As the Sufi mystic Rumi said, all men and women are "cups brimming over with love," conceived in love, sustained in love, destined to return through love to Love Itself.

This alone is the reason for birth. Every woman and man alive on the earth, all those who have ever lived or ever will, are called individually and deliberately into existence by God, endowed with this purpose, this mission, this sacred work. Welcomed on earth by the infinite love of all creation, greeted with open arms by the light of the sun and the moon and the stars, graced with the high, supreme gift of immortality, we all arrive on the earth endowed and prepared for the task. Birth bestows on everyone evenly and equally a holy inheritance, the inheritance of *blessing*—far more "original blessing" than "original sin," as Matthew Fox would say. To fulfill the Divine potential inherent in all this blessedness—and to assist others to fulfill their own—this is the labor of a lifetime, the labor of love.

3

Prayers about birth express the wonder and joy and ecstasy felt in every culture and every heart when a child is born. And even as these prayers revere and honor the miracle of physical birth, they proclaim another birth, a spiritual birth that happens over and over again. This second birth occurs in the innermost core of personal being, in the deepest recesses of the soul, every day of one's life. Here at the most spiritual center of the self, at the ground of one's existence, the little spark of God waits and wants and needs each day to be kindled, tended, nurtured, fed. This spark is the source of Divinity in human life, of the fire and passion and power of love, not just feelings of love, but a sacrificial capacity to serve, to put another first, to hold back so that another may be affirmed.

When the Divine spark in the soul begins to burn, the birth of God—which takes place in eternity and is always taking place in eternity—takes place in time. Meister Eckhart wrote that when this holy birth occurs, we are enabled to see God everywhere, at all times and in all things:

> If [the Divine] birth has truly taken place within you, then no creature can any longer impede your way. All creatures without exception now direct you toward God and toward this birth . . . In whatever you see or hear, in everything, you absorb nothing but this birth. Moreover, everything becomes for you nothing but God. Even

as you stand in the midst of many things and look on these things, your eye sees only God. You grasp God in all.

Finally, fundamentally, this is the work of love: to let the Divine be born in one's own soul, to take one's eyes off oneself and fix one's view on the Eternal in our midst, seeing, revering, praising God in everyone and everything. Like Francis of Assisi, who saw the Divine in sparrows and rabbits and deer; like Simone Weil, who met God in the workers on a Renault assembly line; like Mother Teresa, who finds the Divine in Calcutta on the faces of the poor, one can walk through the world saying every day in every experience of any kind, "This, too, art Thou."

The following prayers show that we are put on earth—"called by name," as Isaiah said—to love and be loved until it is time to return to the Infinite Source of Love from which we came.

On Children

And a woman who held a babe against her bosom said, Speak to us of Children.

And he said:

Your children are not your children.

They are the sons and daughters of Life's longing for itself.

They come through you but not from you,

And though they are with you yet they belong not to you.

You may give them your love but not your thoughts,

For they have their own thoughts.

You may house their bodies but not their souls,

For their souls dwell in the house of tomorrow, which you cannot visit, not even in your dreams.

You may strive to be like them, but seek not to make them like you.

For life goes not backward nor tarries with yesterday.

You are the bows from which your children as living arrows are sent forth.

The archer sees the mark upon the path of the infinite, and He bends you with His might that His arrows may go swift and far.

Let your bending in the archer's hand be for gladness;

For even as He loves the arrow that flies, so He loves also the bow that is stable.

Kahlil Gibran; Lebanon, 1883–1931

THANKS FOR THE BIRTH OF A BABY

O Creator, who dost all human beings create,
Thou hast a great worth on us conferred
By bringing us this little child!

Kenya; oral tradition

BIRTH BAPTISM

The little drop of the Father
  On thy little forehead, beloved one.

The little drop of the Son
  On thy little forehead, beloved one.

The little drop of the Spirit
  On thy little forehead, beloved one.

To aid thee from the fays,
  To guard thee from the host;

To aid thee from the gnome,
  To shield thee from the specter;

To keep thee for the Three,
  To shield thee, to surround thee;

To save thee for the Three,
    To fill thee with the graces;

The little drop of the Three
    To lave thee with the graces.

Celtic oral tradition; collected in Scotland,
nineteenth century

Waiting for a Child

As Sarah longed for Isaac;
  —let the longing for this child increase the longing in our
    hearts that it be another incarnation, a word of God
    enfleshed among us.
As Hannah longed for Samuel;
  —may this baby grow in strength nourished both by love
    and the good health of its mother.
As Elizabeth rejoiced in the babe in her womb;
  —may this child leap with joy and may it encounter the life
    of Jesus in all those who care for it.
As Mary waited in mystery and longing;
  —may this expectant mother experience the joy of bringing
    a new child of God into the world.
As we pray both for the baby and for its mother;
  —grant that we may work for a world where the future is
    secure and where justice is experienced by all.

O God, you have gifted this woman with a fruitful womb,
and we live in expectation for the life that is to be born. As we
await its coming we give thanks to you for bringing us and all
creatures on this earth to birth. May your mothering care and
unconditional love enable this expectant mother to care for

her child as you care for us. May this new child come to know, love, and serve you as did Jesus, who is its companion on the journey home to you. We ask this in his name.
Amen.

Carmelite Nuns of Indiana; United States, twentieth century

DEDICATING A BABY TO GOD

To thee, the Creator, to thee, the Powerful,
I offer this fresh bud,
New fruit of the ancient tree.
Thou art the master, we thy children.
To thee, the Creator, to thee, the Powerful,
Khmvoum (God), *Khmvoum,*
I offer this new plant.

Pygmy prayer; Zaire, traditional

A MOTHER'S PRAYER

Lord,
I was dreaming of success and power,
money and glory,
and here I am immersed,
sometimes trapped,
in my daily routine mothering a family,
feeding, caring for, consoling, listening to . . .
those you entrusted to me,
with machines continuously full of clothes
that have to be emptied,
and refrigerators continuously empty
that have to be filled . . .
So many little deaths to myself,
to my serenity,
to my freedom.
   But you are here!
   alive at the very core of my life
   and you reward each moment I give for love.
An unexpected smile, a look,
and your joy erupts within me
to brighten the thousand daily actions
woven by the thread of life.

Lord, stay with me,
and let the little deaths of each day
lead me along the path
of eternal life.

Christine Gellie; France, twentieth century,
translated by Mary-Theresa McCarthy

For a Safe Delivery: A Husband's and Father's Prayer

ALL ASSEMBLED: O fathers and ancestors, and all who are of the near and far past, bear witness: we cry to thee (God) to let this child be safely born.

HUSBAND: If I have sinned, be merciful, and if thou canst not be merciful, then punish me, slay me: but heal this woman and let this child live.

FATHER *of the woman:* This is my daughter: she is in your hands: spare her life, and give her a living child.

Sierra Leone; oral tradition

FOR LAUREN: A GRANDFATHER'S PRAYER

God of the generations,
this may be more wonderful than I can bear.
Little Lauren, two days old,
lies upon my stomach as I lie upon the couch.
We are concerned because she has not wished to eat yet.
All she wants to do is sleep,
her tiny mouth on a warm spot on my chest.

We breathe together, grandpa and grandchild,
our lives stretching backward and forward
into occasions only I have known,
into occasions only she will know,
into occasions we shall know together.

In this brief time Lauren has been with us
I have come to love her with all my life.
I would fight all beasts barehanded to keep her safe.
I would stay awake every night
so she would not wake up and be alone.
I would work two jobs and eat only gruel
for her to have what she needs.
In truth, what I will do is pray.

❖ ❖ ❖

I pray for Lauren,
that each of her days brings moments of joy
like the joy this moment brings me.
I pray for her mother and father,
that their elation may see them through
And I pray for peace on earth,
for goodness in the world,
for secure and plenteous futures
for all the little ones now being born.

And because of what I have seen and heard
in these years you have been pleased to give me,
I pray for a knowing, compassionate toughness
for every child who enters our difficult world.

Robert Jones; United States, twentieth century

THE BLESSING AFTER THE CIRCUMCISION

Our God and God of our fathers, preserve this child to his father and to his mother, and let his name be called in Israel _____, the son of _____. Let the father rejoice in his offspring, and the mother be glad with the fruit of her body; as it is written, Let thy father and thy mother rejoice, and let her that bore thee be glad: and it is said, And I passed by thee, and I saw thee weltering in thy blood, and I said unto thee, In thy blood live. Yea, I said unto thee, In thy blood live. And it is said, God hath remembered His covenant for ever, the word which He commanded to a thousand generations; the covenant which He made with Abraham, and His oath unto Isaac, and established it unto Jacob for a statute to Israel for an everlasting covenant. And it is said, And Abraham circumcised his son Isaac when he was eight days old, as God had commanded him. O give thanks unto the Lord; for God is good; for his loving-kindness endureth for ever. This little child, _____, may he become great. Even as he has entered into the covenant, so may he enter into the Torah, the nuptial canopy, and into good deeds.

Traditional Jewish prayer

This Fresh Plant: A Bahá'í Prayer

O God! Rear this little babe in the bosom of Thy love and give it milk from the breast of Thy Providence. Cultivate this fresh plant in the rosegarden of Thy love and aid it to grow through the showers of Thy bounty. Make it a child of the Kingdom and lead it to Thy heavenly realm. Thou art powerful and kind, and Thou art the Bestower, the Generous, the Lord of surpassing bounty.

'Abdu'l-Bahá; Iran, 1844–1921

FOR MY BABY

O Lord, my God,
shine the warm light of Your love on my child.
Hold her safe from all illness and harm.
Come into her little soul
and comfort her with Your happiness.
Let her feel your peace.
She is too tiny to speak to me,
and her cooing and gurgles
are hard to translate into human words.
But to You, her little sounds are prayers.
Her cries are cries for Your blessing and grace.
Let her learn Your ways while she is still a child.
In adulthood, let her live the whole span of a human life,
fulfilling Your purposes.
And in her old age, let her die joyfully,
secure in the knowledge of Your eternal love.
I am not asking that she should be wealthy or famous,
but I do ask that she will live prayerfully,
serve others in true humility, loving You.
Smile on her, my God.
    Amen.

Johann Starck; Germany, 1680–1756

From the Ritual Bath of the Newborn in Mexico

. . . O eagle, O tiger, O valiant one, O my grandchild!

Receive and take the water of the Lord of the World, the water which is our life, which makes the body grow and invigorates it and which serves to wash and purify. I pray that this water of celestial blue, clear blue, enter into your body and live in it. I pray that it destroy and carry away from you every ill and all the adversities that were joined in you from the beginning of the world, for we men are entrusted into her hands, she being our mother, Chalchiuhtlicue . . .

Lord, thou seest here your creature that you have sent into this place . . . which is the world. Grant it, O Lord, your gifts and your breath, for thou art the great God . . .

Lady who art mother of the heavens and who is called Citlaltonac and also Citlalicue, to thee my words are directed. I implore thee to give, impress upon, and inspire this, your creature, with your power, whatever it may be . . .

O Lords, celestial gods and goddesses who dwell on high, this is your creature: Deign to implant in it your power and to blow your breath into it in order that it have life upon earth.

Mexico; pre-Hispanic oral tradition

Into This Vast Mystery

I was not aware of the moment when I first crossed the threshold of this life.

What was the power that made me open out into this vast mystery like a bud in the forest at midnight!

When in the morning I looked upon the light I felt in a moment that I was no stranger in this world, that the inscrutable without name and form had taken me in its arms in the form of my own mother.

Even so, in death the same unknown will appear as ever known to me. And because I love this life, I know I shall love death as well.

The child cries out when from the right breast the mother takes it away, in the very next moment to find in the left one its consolation.

Rabindranath Tagore; India, 1861–1941

To Tiráwa: To Bless This Child

When I sing this song,
I pray to Tiráwa
to come down and touch with his breath
the symbol of his face
and all the other symbols on the little child.
I pray with all my spirit
that Tiráwa atius will let the child grow up
and become strong,
and find favor in his life . . .

All that I have been doing to you, little child,
has been a prayer
to call down the breath of Tiráwa atius
to give you long life and strength
and to teach you that you belong to him—
that you are his child
and not mine.

From the Pawnee ceremony for blessing a Child;
Native America, oral tradition

Welcome to My Firstborn

Mother/Father-God
As my door opens and she is brought to me
I rejoice in gratitude,
At this tiny miracle
Wrapped in a blanket,
Eyes closed inward in sleep,
So as to prolong her dream.
Here in the curve of my arm
I soon must wake and nurse her.
Yet I too wait to gaze,
Hushed, in awe;

As wave on wave of joy sweep over me,
I marvel at my baby's starfish hands
Shell-like ears and moss-soft hair
That frames her tiny star-shaped face;
Reminders that she came from me,
But her soul traveled through sky and many waters.
She is a mystery that landed here,
And soon will wake, hungry and eager,
For new life in our world.
Great Creator—Parent of Compassion,

You have entrusted your masterpiece
To my unskilled care—Empower and ready
Me, I pray—and mostly
Let my love that welcomes and enfolds her
Grow as she grows,
So both of us and all of us may
Know and trust and always turn to You,
Source of all Love.

Anita Wheatcroft; United States, twentieth century

A Father's Prayer Feeding His Newborn

I feed you with the wisdom of honey. I feed you with ghee, the gift of God, the beautiful. May you have long life, protected by the Gods, may you live in this world a hundred circling years!

May God grant you intelligence, may God's power grant you intelligence, may God's two divine Messengers, lotus-wreathed, grant to you intelligence.

The Lord is full of life: through firewood God is full of life. By this vital power I make you full of life. The Divine drink is full of life. Through herbs God is full of life.

Kalpa Sūtras, Āśvalāyaṇa Griya Sutra, *I, 15, 1–2; India, c. 600 B.C.E., translated by Raimond Panikkar*

CHRISTMAS CAROL

. . . This night is the eve of the great Nativity,
Born is the Son of Mary the Virgin,
The soles of His feet have reached the earth,
The Son of glory down from on high,
Heaven and earth glowed to Him,
   All hail! let there be joy!

The peace of earth to Him, the joy of heaven to Him,
Behold His feet have reached the world;
The homage of a King be His, the welcome of a Lamb
be His,
King all victorious, Lamb all glorious,
Earth and ocean illumed to Him,
   All hail! let there be joy! . . .

Celtic oral tradition; collected in Scotland, nineteenth century

THE DIVINE BIRTH IN THE SOUL

Pay attention now to exactly where this birth takes place:
This eternal birth
takes place in the soul
totally in the manner
in which it takes place in eternity,
neither more nor less.
There is only one birth—
and this birth takes place in the being
and in the ground and core
of the soul.

Meister Eckhart; Germany, c. 1260–1327,
version by Matthew Fox

COMING OF AGE

In a Hindu rite of initiation thousands of years old, the youth coming of age is clothed in a new white garment, given a cord to tie around the waist, a sacred thread to lay across the shoulder, and a deerskin. Priests in long white robes recite and chant prayers asking that the neophyte may be granted fullness of spirit and a holy life:

> May you be noble . . . may you know the Vedas that you may acquire insight and faith, and keep what you have learned, that you may be endowed with goodness and shining purity.

Accepting a hand-carved wooden staff, the youth symbolically assumes responsibility for his or her own life, for spiritual and moral self-governance, relinquishing the child's dependence on parents and authority figures in favor of self-reliance and leadership of others. Then, heaping wood on a crackling fire, the initiate prays:

> O Lord Agni, the glorious one, make me glorious, as you, gracious Lord, are glorious . . . May I be a custodian of Sacred Knowledge for humanity . . . may I be set ablaze with life, intelligence and vigor . . . may I be

capable of insight . . . may I integrate everything into the cosmic dynamism of sacrifice. *Svaha!*

At the end of the ceremony, the initiate, now a young adult, purified, consecrated, formally confirmed in the ancestral faith, has the privilege of entering into the period of Vedic study.

In most aboriginal cultures, initiation means initiation into pain. Indigenous peoples impose hardship on the young person coming of age—physically, emotionally, and spiritually challenging ordeals—to test and encourage strength and endurance, and to make an impact on the young psyche that will never be forgotten. Harsh and perilous, these wilderness rituals craft a spirit worthy of immortality, a character worthy of ancestorhood.

One Native American rite of passage calls for a period of isolation, three days and nights spent in uninterrupted solitude, without food or protection or distraction—the aloneness itself a trial by fire for one reared in tribal community. With nothing to do but reflect and pray, the initiate waits for counsel from the Great Spirit in the form of a dream or vision. Forged in the context of such sacred terrors as the darkness of night, exposure to the elements, hunger, cold, and loneliness, the initiatory dream images are taken very seriously and serve as guidance for the rest of life.

Initiatory rites and prayers worldwide foster appreciation

of intergenerational cooperation—of the indissoluble bond of love, of giving and receiving—which unites each generation to the preceding and succeeding ones in the vast spiraling history of humankind. A story of breathtaking beauty by the Vietnamese monk Thich Nhat Hanh illustrates the oneness and interconnectedness, the mutuality and depth of caring, that relate all generations to one another:

I have a friend who is an artist. He has been away from home for nearly forty years. He told me that every time he misses his mother all he has to do is look at his hand and he feels better. His mother, a traditional Vietnamese woman, could read only a few Chinese characters and had never studied Western philosophy or science. Before he left Vietnam, she held his hand and told him, "Whenever you miss me, look into your hand, my child. You will see me immediately." How penetrating these simple, sincere words! For nearly forty years, he has looked into his hands many times.

The presence of his mother is not just genetic. Her spirit, her hopes, and her life are also present to him. I know that my friend practices meditation, but I do not know whether he has chosen as his subject "Looking into your hand . . ." This subject can take him far in his practice. From his hand, he can penetrate deeply into the reality of beginningless and endless time. He will be able to see that thousands of generations before him and thousands of generations after him are all he. From time immemorial until the present moment, his life has never been interrupted and his hand is still there, a beginning-less and endless reality.

Prayers for coming of age remind both initiate and initiator that the older generation transmits to the younger not only its highest values, knowledge, and wisdom, but the human spirit itself.

Haftarah for a Covenant of Comforting

You, My people, burnt in fire,
still staring blinded
by the flame and smoke
that rose from Auschwitz and from Hiroshima;

You, My people,
Battered by the earthquakes,
on a planet in convulsion;

You, My people,
Drowning in the flood of words and images
That beckon you to eat and eat,
to drink and drink,
to fill and overfill
your bellies
at the tables of
the gods of wealth and power,

You, My people,
Drowning in the flood of words and images
That—poured unceasing on your eyes and ears—

drown out My words of Torah,
My visions of the earth made whole;

Be comforted:

I have for you a mission full of joy.
I call you to a task of celebration.
I call you to make from fire not an all-consuming blaze
But the light in which all beings see each other fully.
All different,
All bearing One Spark.
I call you to light a flame to see more clearly
That the earth and all who live as part of it
Are not for burning:
A flame to see
The rainbow
in the many-colored faces
of all life.

I call you:
I, the Breath of Life,
Within you and beyond,
Among you and beyond,
That One Who breathes from redwood into grizzly,
That One Who breathes from human into swampgrass,
That One Who breathes the great pulsations of the galaxies.

In every breath You breathe Me,
In every breath I breathe You.

I call You—
In every croak of every frog I call you,
In every rustle of each leaf,
   each life,

I call you,
In the wailings of the wounded earth
I call you.

I call you to a peoplehood renewed:
I call you to reweave the fabric of your folk
and so to join in healing
the weave of life upon your planet.
I call you to a journey of seven generations.

For seven generations past,
the earth has not been able to make Shabbos.
   And so in your own generation
   You tremble on the verge of Flood.
   Your air is filled with poison.
   The rain, the seas, with poison.
   The earth hides arsenals of poisonous fire,
   Seeds of light surcharged with fatal darkness.

The ice is melting,
The seas are rising,
The air is dark with smoke and rising heat.

And so—I call you to carry to all peoples
the teaching that for seven generations
the earth and all her earthlings learn to rest.

I call you once again
To speak for Me,
To speak for me because I have no voice,
To speak the Name of the One who has no Name,
To speak for all the Voiceless of the planet.

Who speaks for the redwood and the rock,
    the lion and the beetle?

My breath I blow through you into a voicing:
Speak for the redwood and the rock,
the lion and the beetle.

I call you to a task of joy:
For seven generations,
this is what I call for you to do:

To make once more the seasons of your joy
into celebrations of the seasons of the earth;

To welcome with your candles the dark of moon and sun,
To bless with careful chewing
   the fruits of every tree
For when you meet to bless
   the rising juice of life
   in every tree trunk—
I am the Tree of Life.

To live seven days in the open, windy huts,
And call out truth to all who live beside you—
You are part of the weave and breath of life,
You cannot make walls to wall it out.

I call you to a covenant between the generations:
That when you gather for a blessing of your children
as they take on the tasks of new tomorrows,
You say to them, they say to you,
That you are all My prophet
Come to turn the hearts of parents
and of children toward each other,
Lest my earth be smashed in utter desolation.

I call you
To eat what
I
call

kosher:
Food that springs from an earth you do not poison,
Oil that flows from an earth you do not drain,
Paper that comes from an earth you do not slash,
Air that comes from an earth you do not choke.

I call you to speak
to all the peoples,
all the rulers.

I call you to walk forth before all nations,
    to pour out water that is free of poison
    and call them all to clean and clarify the rains of winter.
I call you to beat your willows on the earth
    and shout its healing to all peoples.

I call on you to call on all the peoples
to cleanse My Breath, My air,
from all the gases
that turn My earth into a furnace.

I call you to light the colors of the Rainbow
To raise once more before all eyes
That banner of the covenant between Me,
and all the children of Noah and Naamah,
and all that lives and breathes upon the earth—

So that
never again,
all the days of the earth, shall
    sowing and harvest,
    cold and heat,
    summer and winter,
    day and night
    ever cease!

I call you to love the Breath of Life —
    For love is the fire
    That blazes in the Rainbow.

I call you so to live for seven generations
As in the days when you went forth from slavery;
So in these seven generations
The earth will bring forth manna,
The bread of joy and freedom —
and all earth can sing together
Songs of Shabbos.

Arthur Waskow; United States, twentieth century

43

THE GREAT SPIRIT SAYS THAT HE LOVES YOU

Now is the time when He hears us,
He hears us all,
the One who made the Medéwiwin.
Now listen to me,
to what I am about to say to you.
If you take heed of what I say to you,
you shall continue your life always.
Today I make known to you the Great Spirit,
and what He says.

This is what the Great Spirit says:
It is that He loves you.

That which the Great Spirit says,
I impart it to you.
My child,
this knowledge shall give you life.

Algonkin oral tradition; Native America

HEAR, O ISRAEL

Hear, O Israel,
the Lord Our God, the Lord is One.
And you shall love the Lord your God
with all your heart, with all your soul, with all your might,
And these words which I command to you this day
shall be upon your heart.
And you shall teach them to your children
and shall talk of them when you sit in your house,
and when you walk by the way,
and when you lie down,
and when you rise.

Deuteronomy 6:4–7

A Prayer of Saint Paul

May God give you His power
through His Spirit
for your hidden self to grow strong,
so that Christ may live in your heart
through faith, and then,
planted in love and built on love,
you will with all the saints have strength
to grasp the breadth and the length,
the height and the depth, until,
knowing the love of Christ,
which is beyond all
knowledge,
you are filled with the utter fullness of God.
Glory be to God whose power,
working in us,
can do infinitely more than we can ask or imagine;
glory be to God from generation to generation
in the Church and in Christ Jesus for ever and ever.
Amen.

Ephesians 3:16–21

The Exordium

In the Name of Allah
The Compassionate
The Merciful

Praise be to Allah, Lord of all Creation,
The Compassionate, the Merciful,
King of Judgment Day!
You alone we worship, and to You alone
we pray for help.
Guide us along the straight path
The path of those whom You have blessed,
Not of those against whom there is disfavor
Nor of those who have gone astray.

The Koran; 1:1–7

Go Forth in a Holy Manner: A Sioux Girl Comes of Age

White-Buffalo-Cow-Woman-Appears, you have prayed to *Wakan-Tanka*, the Great Spirit, you will now go forth among your people in a holy manner, and you will be an example to them. You will cherish those things which are most sacred in the universe; you will be as Mother Earth — humble and fruitful. May your steps, and those of your children, be firm and sacred! As *Wakan-Tanka* has been merciful to you, so you, too, must be merciful to others, especially to those children who are without parents. If such a child should ever come to your lodge, and if you should have but one piece of meat, you should give it to her. You should be as generous as this! As I now place this meat in your mouth, we should all remember how merciful *Wakan-Tanka* is in providing for our wants. In the same manner you must provide for your children! . . .

Hee-ay-hay-ee-ee! Grandfather, *Wakan-Tanka*, behold them! These people and all the generations to come are Yours. Look upon this virgin, White-Buffalo-Cow-Woman-Appears, who has been purified and honored this good day. May Your Light which never fails be upon her always and upon all her relatives!

From a Sioux rite of initiation of a young woman;
Native America, oral tradition

One with the Light of Dawn: A Sioux Boy Comes of Age

O You four Powers of the universe, you wingeds of the air, and all the peoples who move in the universe—you have all been placed in the pipe. Help this young man with the knowledge which has been given to all of you by *Wakan-Tanka*. Be merciful to him! O *Wakan-Tanka*, grant that this young man may have relatives; that he may be one with the four winds, the four Powers of the world, and with the light of the dawn. May he understand his relationship with all the winged peoples of the air. He will place his feet upon the sacred earth of a mountaintop; may he receive understanding there; may his generations to come be holy! All things give thanks to You, O *Wakan-Tanka*, who are merciful and who help us all. We ask all this of You because we know that You are the only One, and that You have power over all things!

From a Sioux rite of initiation of a young man;
Native America, oral tradition

The Ocean Is So Wide

O, God,
O, God, be with me.
For the ocean is so wide,
and my boat is so small.

Author unknown; Brittany, France, oral tradition

As a Young Tree

You must grow again into the image of God both from above and from below. Be as a young tree which is moved by the wind and must stand in heat and cold. In such turmoil, it draws its power to itself above and below and must endure many wind storms and stand in great danger before it can become a tree that bears fruit. In such turmoil the sun's power moves in it, the wild characteristics of the tree are pressed through and tinctured by the sun's power, and by this the tree grows.

From the Safed Kabbalist tradition;
ancient Galilee, sixteenth century

GO FORWARD SECURELY

What you hold, may you always hold.
What you do, may you always do and never abandon.
But with swift pace, light step,
   and unswerving feet,
   so that even your steps stir up no dust,
go forward
   securely, joyfully, and swiftly,
on the path of prudent happiness,
   believing nothing,
   agreeing with nothing
   which would dissuade you from this resolution
   or which would place a stumbling block for you on the way,
   so that you may offer your vows to the Most High
in the pursuit of that perfection
to which the Spirit of the Lord has called you.

Clare of Assisi; Italy, 1194–1253

LET US WORK

Therefore, let us work, let us develop all our possibilities; not for ourselves, but for our fellow-creatures. Let us be enlightened in our efforts, let us strive after the general welfare of humanity and indeed of all creation. We are born here to do certain things. Life may be misery or not; it concerns us not; let us do what we have to do. We are not here wholly alone . . . we cannot save ourselves unless others are saved. We cannot advance unless the general progress is assured. We must help one another, we must abandon our vulgar egocentric ideas, we must expand ourselves so that the whole universe is identified with us, and so that our interests are those of humanity. The attainment of Nirvana and the manifestation of the Buddhist life are possible only through the denial of selfhood and through the united labor of all our brother creatures.

Soyen Shaku; Japan, 1859–1919

Go Now, My Friend

My friend,

You are sent to be

    Light-bearer
    Bread-giver

To bear in your eyes the light that has broken
Through the darkness and pain of your journey
So that others may find the way to their destiny:

To carry in your hands the warm bread
You have kneaded in love
So that others may be fed to satiety.

Go now, my friend,

    Give away the candle
    Give away the bread

And be

Candle.
Bread.

Brother Thomas More Page; United States,
twentieth century

To Possess All, Desire Nothing

To reach satisfaction in all
  desire its satisfaction in nothing.
To come to possess all
  desire the possession of nothing.
To arrive at being all
  desire to be nothing.
To come to the knowledge of all
  desire the knowledge of nothing.
To come to the pleasure you have not
  you must go by a way in which you enjoy not.
To come to the knowledge you have not
  you must go by a way in which you know not.
To come to the possession you have not
  you must go by a way in which you possess not.
To come to be what you are not
  you must go by a way in which you are not.
When you turn toward something
  you cease to cast yourself upon the all.
For to go from all to the all
  you must deny yourself of all in all.

And when you come to the possession of the all
   you must possess it without wanting anything.
Because if you desire to have something in all
   your treasure in God is not purely your all.

Saint John of the Cross; Spain, 1542–1591

THE COUNSEL OF A MAYA SAGE

You are to wander,
entering and departing
from strange villages . . .
Perhaps you will achieve nothing anywhere.
It may be that the things you carry with you
and your items of trade
find no favor in any place . . .
But do not turn back, keep a firm step . . .
Something you will achieve;
Something the Lord of the Universe will assign to you.

Chilam Balam, Maya priest; Yucatán Peninsula,
pre-Hispanic oral tradition

CHRIST EVERYWHERE

May the strength of God guide me this day, and may
God's power preserve me.
May the wisdom of God instruct me: the eye of God
watch over me; the ear of God hear me; the word of
God give sweetness to my speech; the hand of God
defend me; and may I follow the way of God.
    Christ be with me, Christ before me,
    Christ be after me, Christ within me,
    Christ beneath me, Christ above me,
    Christ at my right hand, Christ at my left,
    Christ in the fort, Christ in the chariot,
    Christ in the ship
    Christ in the heart of everyone who thinks of me,
    Christ in the mouth of everyone who speaks to me.
    Christ in every eye that sees me.
    Christ in every ear that hears me.

Said to be on Saint Patrick's breastplate;
Celtic tradition, first millennium C.E.

MAY HE BECOME A MAN

My Sun!
My Morning Star!
Help this child to become a man.
I name him
Rain-dew falling!
I name him
Star Mountain!

Native America; Tewa oral tradition

Give Me Someone

Lord,
when I am famished,
  give me someone who needs food;
when I am thirsty,
  send me someone who needs water;
when I am cold,
  send me someone to warm;
when I am hurting,
  send me someone to console;
when my cross becomes heavy,
  give me another's cross to share;
when I am poor,
  lead someone needy to me;
when I have no time,
  give me someone to help for a moment;
when I am humiliated,
  give me someone to praise;
when I am discouraged,
  send me someone to encourage;
when I need another's understanding,
  give me someone who needs mine;

when I need somebody to take care of me,
   send me someone to care for;
when I think of myself,
   turn my thoughts toward another.

Anonymous; Japan, twentieth century,
translated by Mary-Theresa McCarthy

The Supreme Good Is Like Water

The supreme good is like water,
which nourishes all things without trying to.
It is content with the low places that people disdain.
Thus it is like the Tao.

In dwelling, live close to the ground.
In thinking, keep to the simple.
In conflict, be fair and generous.
In governing, don't try to control.
In work, do what you enjoy.
In family life, be completely present.

When you are content to be simply yourself
and don't compare or compete,
everybody will respect you.

From the Tao Te Ching, *Lao-tzu; China, c. 604–531 B.C.E.,*
translated by Stephen Mitchell

SONG OF THE EARTH SPIRIT

It is lovely indeed, it is lovely indeed.
I, I am the spirit within the earth . . .
The feet of the earth are my feet . . .
The legs of the earth are my legs . . .
The bodily strength of the earth is my strength . . .
The thoughts of the earth are my thoughts . . .
The voice of the earth is my voice . . .
The feather of the earth is my feather . . .
All that belongs to the earth belongs to me . . .
All that surrounds the earth surrounds me . . .
I, I am the sacred words of the earth . . .
It is lovely indeed, it is lovely indeed.

Native America; Navajo oral tradition

INITIATION INTO VEDIC STUDY

May the Goddess who spun, who wove, who measured and fashioned this garment, clothe you with long life! Be endowed with strength, splendor, and long life. May you live to old age! Put on this garment. Be a protector of mankind against menacing speeches. Be a protector of your friends against the curses of men. Live a hundred years, full of vigor and increasing wealth. May you be noble, blessed with fullness of life, sharing generously your wealth. May you know the Vedas that you may acquire insight and faith, and keep what you have learned, that you may be endowed with goodness and shining purity.

The Initiate responds:

This staff which is falling from the sky upon the earth I now take up, with prayer for life, fullness of spirit, and the splendor of *Brahman*.

O Lord, the glorious one, make me glorious, as you, glorious Lord, yourself are glorious. As you, Lord, are custodian of sacrifice for the Gods, even so may I be custodian of Sacred Knowledge for humanity. As you, O Lord, are set ablaze by

wood, so may I be set ablaze by life, intelligence and vigor
. . . May I be capable of insight, not obstructive. May I increase in honor and divine glory. May I integrate everything
into the cosmic dynamism of the sacrifice. *Svaha!*

Gṛhya Sūtras; *India, c. 600 B.C.E.*,
translated by Raimond Panikkar

HELP YOUNG PEOPLE!

Lord, the world needs
   this marvelous wealth which is youth.
   Help young people!
   They hold the inexhaustible wealth of the future . . .
   Do not allow an easy life to corrupt them
   Nor obstacles to crush their spirit.
   Free them from the worst danger of all—
   That of getting used to being
   Old within themselves
   And only young on the outside.

Dom Helder Camara; Brazil, 1909–

The Path

This is the path. There is no other that leads to vision. Go on this path, and you will confuse MARA, the devil of confusion.

Whoever goes on this path travels to the end of his sorrow. I showed this path to the world when I found the roots of sorrow.

It is you who must make the effort. The Great of the past only show the way. Those who think and follow the path become free from the bondage of MARA.

All is transient. When one sees this, he is above sorrow. This is the clear path.

All is sorrow. When one sees this, he is above sorrow. This is the clear path.

All is unreal. When one sees this, he is above sorrow. This is the clear path.

If a man when young and strong does not arise and strive when he should arise and strive, and thus sinks into laziness and lack of determination, he will never find the path of wisdom.

A man should control his words and mind and not do any harm with his body. If these ways of action are pure, he can make progress on the path of the wise.

The Dhammapada, *274–281; Southeast Asia, compiled c. third century B.C.E., translated by Juan Mascaró*

May Kindly Columba Guide You

And now, may kindly Columba guide you
To be an isle in the sea,
To be a hill on the shore,
To be a star in the night,
To be a staff for the weak.
Amen.

*Celtic oral tradition; Ireland, Britain, Scotland,
Wales, first millennium,* C.E.

CONFRONTING ILLNESS

A pearl of impenetrable mystery lies at the heart of all illness, sickness, and disease, wounds, injuries, and handicaps, concealing—perhaps forever—a holy secret, something incomprehensible, probably unknowable. Subtly present wherever, whenever, however the perfect wholeness which God wills for all humanity is lacking or damaged, the strange secret hides at the burning depths of Divine Existence, far beyond the physician's science and art, the healer's skills, the shaman's powers, the ill person's ability to understand. The dark truth about healing, about recovery, about restoration of full health, remains in the waning twentieth century as obscure as it was in the Middle Ages. Something there is that no medicine, no meditation, no act of self-help, no "alternative" medical treatment, and—more important—neither faith nor prayer can cure.

A bright stream of wisdom courses through the world's prayers about illness and healing in the slender phrase "if it be Thy will." Implicit or explicit, these five words add a notion that is elemental in the spiritual life: "Not my will, but Yours." Prayers asking for recovery assume that every human effort will be made, that all medical, psychological, and spiritual resources, knowledge, and skills will be employed to the fullest extent possible to bring about a cure. Then, when all that is done, prayers petitioning God for a cure, wisely add the condition, "if it be Thy will."

God is always with us, God is always active within us, and yet the cure may not be granted; the healing may never take place. The Fourth Psalm, especially Stephen Mitchell's exquisite interpretation, prays in the only way one can:

> *Even in the midst of great pain, Lord,*
> *I praise You for that which is.*
> *I will not refuse this grief*
> *or close myself to this anguish.*
> *Let shallow men pray for ease:*
> *"Comfort us; shield us from sorrow."*
> *I pray for whatever you send me,*
> *and I ask to receive it as your gift.*
> *You have put a joy in my heart*
> *greater than all the world's riches.*
> *I lie down trusting the darkness,*
> *for I know that even now you are here.*

Here, calm acceptance of affliction liberates the spirit to communicate intimately with God. The Psalmist has so thoroughly surrendered to "that which is," to his situation, to reality, that he can face the darkness of night in peace, without fear. "You are here," he prays. You are all I need.

Advancing beyond that already high spiritual plane to the

highest possible plane, the Psalmist is able to speak words of praise—praise for God and for life—"even in the midst of great pain." For prayer, while it holds no guarantee of healing, promises, always and unconditionally: love, solace, trust, and hope.

Tomorrow I Shall Die

I thank You, my God, for the care You have lavished upon me all my life. For six long months, I have been lying on my bed, my body tormented by illness. I lie in chains like a prisoner to this disease. My energy is gone; I have no strength. From my head to my feet, weakness has settled in, binding me to this bed. Like a blind person, I no longer see the green world. For half a year, I have seen only the walls of my little hut, and they are growing dim.

Have You nailed me to Your Cross? Is this sickness a crucifixion?

Yet You have brought me joyfully to this place, and I give You thanks. Tomorrow I shall die. This lash on my body shall cease; I shall meet You face to face. I shall be at peace. Darkness already shrouds my body, but in my soul shines light. Today tears fall from my eyes, but my soul already tastes the sweetness of Your love.

I am no more than a tiny field mouse, caught in the claws of a cat. But tomorrow I shall be free as a springtime breeze.

The sins of my life are great, far more huge than this pain. But tomorrow I shall be with You, whose forgiveness is infinite, eternally.

Anonymous; British Isles, c. sixth century

In Depression

O God, You care for Your creation with tenderness. In the midst of the greatest pain, You offer hope. We are praying for our loved one, _____, whose spirit is lost, whose soul is in despair. She curses the day she came into life and longs for oblivion.

Let her feel Your pure love. Let her believe in the miracle of rebirth so that she can experience now a foretaste of the joy she will know in eternity. Amen.

Dimma, a Christian monk; Ireland, seventh century

When I Go from Hence

When I go from hence let this be my parting word, that what I have seen is unsurpassable.

I have tasted of the hidden honey of this lotus that expands on the ocean of light, and thus am I blessed — let this be my parting word.

In this playhouse of infinite forms I have had my play and here have I caught sight of him that is formless.

My whole body and my limbs have thrilled with this touch beyond touch; and if the end comes here, let it come — let this be my parting word.

Rabindranath Tagore; India, 1861–1941

I Am Afflicted

My back is broken by the conflict of my thoughts;
O Beloved One, come and stroke my head in mercy!
The palm of Thy hand on my head gives me rest,
Thy hand is a sign of Thy bounteous providence,
Remove not Thy shadow from my head,
I am afflicted, afflicted, afflicted!
Sleep has deserted my eyes
Through my longing for Thee, O Envy of cypresses! . . .
O take my life, Thou art the Source of Life!
For apart from Thee I am wearied of my life.
I am a lover well versed in lovers' madness,
I am weary of learning and sense.

Jalal-ud-Din Rumi; Persia, 1207–1273

For Those Who Are Sick

Thy name is my healing, O my God, and remembrance of Thee is my remedy. Nearness to Thee is my hope, and love for Thee is my companion. Thy mercy to me is my healing and my succor in both this world and the world to come. Thou verily art the All-Bountiful, the All-Knowing, the All-Wise.

Bahá'u'lláh; Iran, 1817–1892

For Those Who Care for the Sick

Lord, I am grateful to You
that in Your mysterious love
You have taken away from me
all earthly wealth,
and that You now clothe and feed me
through the kindness of others.

Lord, I am grateful to You
that since You have taken away from me
the sight of my eyes,
You care for me now
through the eyes of others.

Lord, I am grateful to You
that since you have taken away from me
the strength of my hands and heart,
you care for me now
through the hands and hearts of others.

Lord, I pray for them,
that You will reward them in Your love,

that they may continue to faithfully serve and
  care
until they come to a happy end
in eternity with You.

Mechthild of Magdeburg; Germany, c. 1210–1280

Night Chant

Lord of the Mountains!

My feet restore Thou for me.
My legs restore Thou for me.
My body restore Thou for me.

My voice Thou restorest for me.
Restore all for me in beauty.
Make beautiful all that is before me.
Make beautiful all that is behind me.

It is done in beauty.
It is done in beauty.
It is done in beauty.
It is done in beauty.

Native America; Navajo oral tradition

LITANY FOR A SICK CHILD

MOTHER: O spirits of the past, this little one I hold is my child: she is your child also. Therefore, be gracious unto her.

WOMEN, *chanting:* She has come into a world of trouble: sickness is in the world, cold and pain: the pain you knew: the sickness with which you were familiar.

MOTHER: Let her sleep in peace, for there is healing in sleep: let none among you be angry with me or with my child.

WOMEN: Let her grow: let her become strong: let her become full-grown: then will she offer such a sacrifice to you that will delight your hearts.

Sierra Leone; oral tradition

Vedic Prayer for Recovery

Guard well, O Man, your share of immortality, that you may reach old age without mishap. Spirit and life I now impart to you! Do not vanish into shadow and darkness! Do not perish.

Go forth, I adjure you, into the light of the living. I draw you toward a life of a hundred autumns. Releasing you from the bonds of death and malediction, I stretch forth your life thread into the distant future.

From the Wind I have taken your breath, from the Sun your eyesight. I strengthen your heart in you, consolidate your limbs. I adjure you to speak with tongue free from stammering.

With the breath that dwells in creatures of two legs or four, I blow upon you as one blows on a fire just kindled.
Let him live, not die! This man we now revive. I bring him healing. O Death, do not strike this man.

Speak in his favor! Seize him not, but release him, yours though he be. Let him stay here with all his strength! Have mercy upon him, O powers of destruction, protect him! Grant to him fullness of days, removing all evil!

Bless this man, O Death, have mercy upon him! Let him rise and depart, safe and sound, with unimpaired hearing! May he reach a hundred years and enjoy life's blessings!

We rescue him, Death, from your murky path which admits of no return, and, protecting him from the descent, we make a shield to guard him—this is our prayer.

To you I now impart in-breath and out-breath, a ripe old age, death at its close, well-being!

India, Atharva Veda, *VIII; c. 2500 B.C.E.*

I WILL LIFT UP MINE EYES

I will lift up mine eyes unto the hills
from whence cometh my help,
My help cometh from the Lord,
which made heaven and earth.
He will not suffer thy foot to be moved: He that keepeth
    thee will not slumber.
Behold, He that keepeth Israel shall neither slumber nor
    sleep.
The Lord is thy keeper:
the Lord is thy shade upon thy right hand.
The sun shall not smite thee by day,
nor the moon by night.
The Lord shall preserve thee from all evil:
He shall preserve thy soul.
The Lord shall preserve thy going out and thy coming in
from this time forth, and even for evermore.

Psalm 121

The Medical Oath

Your eternal providence has appointed me to watch over the life and health of your creatures. May the love for my art actuate me at all times; may neither avarice nor miserliness nor the thirst for glory or for a great reputation engage my mind . . . May I never see in a patient anything but a fellow creature in pain. Grant me strength, time, and opportunity always to correct what I have acquired, always to extend its domain, for knowledge is immense and the spirit of man can always extend indefinitely to enrich itself daily with new requirements . . .

O God, you have appointed me to watch over the life and death of your creatures. Here I am, ready for my vocation.

Moses Maimonides; Spain, 1135–1204

A MEDICAL STUDENT'S PRAYER AT HER FIRST ENCOUNTER WITH DEATH

Thank you, Mr. Sambhav,
for sharing your death.
My life meanders through yours
and wonders at each fiber.
In breath you forged a way;
In your stillness I am born to my path.

Tara Grabowsky; United States,
twentieth century

OUT OF THE DEPTHS

Out of the depths I cry to Thee,
  O Lord!
O Lord, hear my voice!
Let Thine ears be attentive
  to the voice of my supplications!

If Thou, O Lord, shouldst mark
  iniquities,
    Lord, who could stand?
But there is forgiveness with Thee,
  and I stand before Thee in
  awe.

I wait for the Lord, my soul waits,
  and in God's word I hope;
my soul waits for the Lord
  more than the watchman for the
    coming of the dawn,
  more than the watchman for the
    morning.

❉   ❉   ❉

O Israel, hope in the Lord!
For with God there is
steadfast love,
With the Lord is plenteous
redemption.

Psalm 130

GOD WITHHELD FROM HIM PAIN

In the whole of his life he suffered no headache,
So that he never cried to God, wretch that he was.
God granted him the absolute dominion of the world,
But withheld from him pain and sorrow and cares;
Because pain and sorrow and loads of cares
Are the lot of God's friends in the world.
Pain is better than the dominion of the world,
So that thou mayest call on God in secret.
The cries of those free from pain are dull and cold,
The cries of the sorrowful come from a burning heart.

Jalal-ud-Din Rumi; Persia, 1207–1273

My Voice Is Silent Now

Strengthen me, O Lord,
for your servant is bowed to the dust.
The voice that used to sing Your praise
is silent now . . .
Raise me up, do not leave me alone.
I need my health to sing Your praise,
and help Your people lead holy lives.
I plead with You: You are my
    strength,
do not desert me, do not leave me
    alone.
I grew weak amid the storm,
and betrayed your love,
but I long to return to You.

Gregory of Nazianzus; ancient Cappadocia,
329–389

FOR HELP IN SICKNESS

You, Father God,
Who are in the heavens and below;
Creator of everything and omniscient;
Of the earth and the heavens;
We are but little children
Unknowing anything evil;
If this sickness has been brought by man
We beseech you, help us through these roots.
In case it was inflicted by you, the Conserver,
Likewise do we entreat your mercy on your child;
Also you, our grandparents, who sleep in the place of the
    shades,
We entreat all of you who sleep on one side.
All ancestors, male and female, great and small,
Help us in this trouble, have compassion on us;
So that we also can sleep peacefully . . .
Please listen to our earnest request.

Tanzania; Konda oral tradition

REPOSE OF SLEEP

O God of life, darken not to me Thy light,
O God of life, close not to me Thy joy,
O God of life, shut not to me Thy door,
   O God of life, refuse not to me Thy mercy,
   O God of life, quench Thou to me Thy wrath,
   And O God of life, crown Thou to me Thy gladness,
O God of life, crown Thou to me Thy gladness.

Celtic tradition; collected in Scotland,
nineteenth century

COME FOR ME

Oh, Spirits of the dead,
come for me.
Oh, Murungu,
God of Gikuyu and Mumbi,
Who dwells on high Kerinyaga,
yet is everywhere,
Why don't you
release me from misery?
Dear Mother Earth,
why don't you open
and swallow me up?

Zaire; Pygmy oral tradition

OFFERINGS TO THE GREAT SPIRIT

That which is holy,
   may it become my offering.
That which is good,
   may it become my offering.
The beautiful black bead,
   may it become my offering.
The beautiful sparkling stone,
   may it become my offering.
The beautiful blue pollen,
   may it become my offering.
The beautiful grain of yellow corn,
   may it become my offering.
The beautiful grain of purple corn,
   may it become my offering.
The beautiful white shell,
   may it become my offering.
The beautiful grain of purple corn,
   may it become my offering.
The beautiful grain of yellow corn,
   may it become my offering.
The beautiful blue pollen,
   may it become my offering.

The beautiful sparkling stone,
    may it become my offering.
The beautiful black bead,
    may it become my offering.
That which is good,
    may it become my offering.
That which is holy,
    may it become my offering.

Native America; Navajo oral tradition

In Distress

Hear the call of those
in distress and affliction
beseeching You day and night.
Enlighten those who have forsaken You:
may none of them perish
but may they all recognize the truth.
And may we together
with one heart
and one mind
glorify Your most holy name,
Father, Son, and Holy Spirit,
as it was in the beginning,
is now and ever shall be.

Anonymous Christians; Rumania, twentieth century,
translated by Mary-Theresa McCarthy

I WILL DANCE FOR YOU

Lord,
    give me Your hand
    and I will dance for you.

Out of love for us,
    you took many steps.

You traversed dusty roads in Galilee
    to announce Your Good News.
You did not hesitate on the path leading You
    to the Mount of Olives.
And in the beauty of Your resurrection,
    You revealed Yourself to Your disciples.
You even met some of them
    rather discreetly
    along the road to Emmaus.
To each one
    You expressed Your love and fidelity.
You walked before me along the path
    where You call me today.

In my gloom,
    You will be a light for my steps.

In my frailty,
   You will be the vigor in my heart.
I know that with the glow of Your spirit
   I will dance my death
   and I will leap to You.

*Jacques Dubuc; Quebec, Canada, twentieth century,
translated by Mary-Theresa McCarthy*

LED TO THE DESERT

Consider the divine spirit in the human
    soul.
This spirit is not easily satisfied.
It storms the firmament
and scales the heavens
trying to reach the Spirit that drives the
    heavens.
Because of this energy
everything in the world grows green,
flourishes,
and bursts into leaf.
But the spirit is never satisfied.
It presses on
deeper and deeper into the vortex
further and further into the
    whirlpool,
the primary source
in which the spirit has its origin.
This spirit seeks to be
broken through by God.
    God leads this spirit
into a desert

into the wilderness and solitude of the
    divinity
where God is pure unity
and where God gushes up within himself.

Meister Eckhart; Germany, c. 1260–1327,
version by Matthew Fox

MARRIAGE

Marriage is a sacred relationship. When we make the great decision to take religious vows within the consecrated space of a church or synagogue, temple, shrine, or mosque, in the presence of God and a believing community, we are entering into a holy covenant. Wedding vows express a desire deep in the human heart to cherish and nourish another with one's whole body and mind and soul and spirit through life and death and beyond death for all eternity. Hallowed words from the Christian rite of marriage, "For better or worse, for richer or poorer, in sickness and in health," echo the essence of nuptial promises made in religions all over the world.

The spiritual nature of the rituals with which married life begins indicates the sacredness and longed-for permanence of the marital relationship. Men and women vested with spiritual authority—priests and rabbis, elders, tribal chieftains and ministers—preside at colorful wedding rites and pray with the marrying couple for the grace of lasting love. Golden rings may be exchanged as a symbol and sign that the highest possible value is placed on the dignity and continuity of the marital bond.

The world's nuptial prayers honor the relationship of a

wedded couple as a mirror of God's love for humankind. The partners' union is seen in prayers as a sanctified place for working out one's salvation and growing toward full human wholeness through the miracle of self-giving love. Within such a sacramental framework, two people together can foster the journey of each to God. As Hasidic masters have always taught, the power of prayer "can topple walls": prayer can take us to the deepest and holiest ground of life where it becomes possible to renew our commitment, strengthen love, comfort, and help and forgive.

In *Dialogues with a Modern Mystic*, Andrew Harvey describes exquisitely the unsurpassable rewards of "spiritual marriage":

> The fruit of the spiritual life is that you can, in the end, love another being truly, both in the body and in the soul. To love consciously with your divine self another divine self is one of the highest experiences on the earth. To love consciously with your divine heart, which is boundless and boundlessly tender, another divine heart brings into the core of ordinary life something of what St. John of the Cross called "the tenderness of the life of God."

Sadly, some marriages shatter under the weight of life's sorrows and must come to a premature end. For this reason, this chapter includes—along with prayers extolling the bliss of enduring love — consolation for times of heartbreak, a thousand-year-old blessing for a second marriage, and the sage advice of the great Persian mystic Rumi: "If you have lost heart on the path of love, flee to Me without delay: for I am a fortress invincible."

ON MARRIAGE

Then Almitra spoke again and said, And what of Marriage, master?

And he answered, saying:

You were born together, and together you shall be forever-more.

You shall be together when the white wings of death scatter your days.

Ay, you shall be together even in the silent memory of God.

But let there be spaces in your togetherness,

And let the winds of the heavens dance between you.

Love one another, but make not a bond of love:

Let it rather be a moving sea between the shores of your souls.

Fill each other's cup but drink not from one cup.

Give one another of your bread but eat not from the same loaf.

Sing and dance together and be joyous, but let each one of you be alone,

Even as the strings of a lute are alone though they quiver with the same music.

Give your hearts, but not into each other's keeping.
For only the hand of Life can contain your hearts.
And stand together yet not too near together:
For the pillars of the temple stand apart,
And the oak tree and the cypress grow not in each other's
shadow.

Kahlil Gibran; Lebanon; 1883–1931

LOVERS SHARE A SACRED DECREE

Lovers share a sacred decree to seek the Beloved.
They roll head over heels, rushing towards the Beautiful
    One
Like a torrent of water
In truth everything and everyone is a shadow of the
    Beloved
and our seeking is His seeking and our words are His
    words.
At times we fly toward the Beloved like a dancing stream
At times we are still water held in His pitcher
At times we boil in the pot
Turning to vapor
That is the job of the Beloved
He breathes into my ear until my soul takes on his
    fragrance
He is the soul of my soul
How can I escape?
But why would any soul in this world want to escape from
    the Beloved?
He will melt your pride, making you thin as a strand of hair
Yet do not trade, even for both worlds,
One strand of His hair

We search for Him here and there, while looking right at
    Him
Sitting by his side, we ask: Oh Beloved, where is the
    Beloved?
Enough with such questions,
Let silence take you to the core of life
All your talk is worthless when compared with one whisper
    of the Beloved.

Jalal-ud-Din Rumi; Persia, 1207–1273,
translated by Jonathan Star

WHITHER THOU GOEST, I WILL GO

Intreat me not to leave thee,
   Or to return from following after thee:
For whither thou goest, I will go,
   And where thou lodgest, I will lodge.
Thy people shall be my people,
   And thy God my God.
Where thou diest, will I die,
   And there will I be buried.
The Lord do so to me, and more also,
   If ought but death part me from thee.

Ruth 1:16–17

A Hindu Prayer for Marriage

O Lord, we pray that the holy truth, "God is Love," may be manifest in our sacred union. Grant us the spirit of harmony and self-sacrifice that we may preserve the sacred covenant of our marriage. Grant our marriage the joys of love, liberal wealth, and the perfection of righteousness, that we may be fulfilled and ready for liberation. May our union be a vehicle for great souls to take birth in this world. May our family be a spiritual fortress against the forces of worldliness, that our children may nurture the Divine light of Your Being within them. Give us the will to fulfill our duties as householders, to be mainstays of humanity, nurturers of children, a refuge for the elderly, and a sure support of your renunciate monastics. May our home be always a spiritual haven for our ancestors, our relatives, our guests, whom we will greet as God ourselves, and above all a temple for You, Lord, that we may be ever a channel to the world of Your Peace and Your Love. *Aum shanti, shanti, shanti.*

A renunciate monk; Kauai's Hindu Monastery, Hawaii,
twentieth century

From the Zoroastrian Wedding Ceremony

The twain in one are joined today. May their right hands be tied by the bond of love in lasting union. May the mind of one blend with the mind of the other and the heart be in tune with the heart. May the twin spirits be a composite spirit in joy and sorrow, success and failure, prosperity and adversity. May the two come nearer to each other in Good Thoughts, Good Words, and Good Deeds from day unto day.

May each transmit something good of each to the others. May each take the best that is in the other, and give something better than the best. May each give of one's goodness what the other lacks and give mutual completion to each other in life.

Locked in the embrace of wedded love, may they live for each other, may they share each other's feelings, may they lighten each other's load in life, and may they live in the loving fellowship of minds and hearts. May each elevate and embellish what nature has bestowed on the other. With hearts knitted together, may the two be the whole world to each other. May each one be life for the other. May he be hers and she be his wholly for all the days of their lives. May each cleave faithfully unto each in body and mind and spirit as the vine that twines its tendrils around the tall tree. May better than the best come unto them. May it be so even as we pray, *Ahura Mazda*. Amen.

Anonymous Zoroastrian prayer; Persia, third or fourth century

A MARITAL BLESSING

May the Lord bless you
and may Christ keep you,
and may the Lord show His face to you
and give you peace;
and may Christ fill you with every spiritual blessing
for the forgiveness of sins and for eternal life,
for ever and ever. Amen.

A form of the Aaronic blessing; England, tenth century

Navajo Song of Meeting

Now the Mother Earth
And the Father sky,
   Meeting, joining one another,
   Helpmates ever, they.
      All is beautiful,
      All is beautiful,
      All is beautiful, indeed . . .

Native America; Navajo oral tradition

From the Jewish Rite of Marriage

Blessed art Thou, O Lord our God,
King of the universe,
Who hast created joy and gladness,
bridegroom and bride,
mirth and exultation,
pleasure and delight,
love, community, peace, and fellowship.
Soon may there be heard in the cities of Judah,
and in the streets of Jerusalem,
the voice of joy and gladness,
the voice of the bridegroom and the voice of the bride,
the jubilant voice of the bridegrooms from their canopies,
and of youths from their feasts of song.
Blessed art Thou, O Lord,
who makest the bridegroom to rejoice with the bride.

Traditional Jewish prayer

From the Song of Songs

Rise up, my love, my fair one, and come away.
For, lo, the winter is past,
The rain is over and gone;
The flowers appear on the earth;
The time of the singing of birds is come,
And the voice of the turtle is heard in our land;
The fig tree ripeneth its figs,
And the vine puts forth its blossom,
They give forth fragrance.
Arise, my love, my fair one, and come away.

Song of Songs 2:10–13

By night on my bed
I sought him whom my soul loveth:
I sought him, but found him not.
I called him but he gave no answer.
I said, "I will rise now, and go about the city,
In the streets and in the broad ways,
I will seek him whom my soul loveth":
I sought him, but found him not.
The watchmen that go about the city found me:

To them I said, "Have you seen him whom my soul
    loveth?"
Scarcely had I passed them,
When I found him whom my soul loveth:
I held him, and would not let him go,
Until I had brought him into my mother's house,
And into the chamber of her that conceived me.

Song of Songs 3:1–4

I am my beloved's
And he is mine.
Come, my beloved,
let us go forth into the field;
and lodge in the villages.
Let us go up early to the vineyards;
Let us see whether the vine hath budded,
    whether the grape hath opened,
And the pomegranates are in bloom;
There will I give thee my love.
The mandrakes give forth fragrance,
And at our doors are all manner of precious fruits, new and
    old,
Which I have laid up for thee, O my beloved.

Song of Songs 7:10–13

Set me as a seal upon thine heart,
as a seal upon thine arm:
For love is as strong as death,
jealousy is cruel as the grave:
Its flashes are flashes of fire,
A most vehement flame.
Many waters cannot quench love,
Neither can floods drown it:
If a man would give all the wealth of his house for love
It would be utterly scorned.

Song of Songs 8:6–7

A Medieval Blessing for a Second Marriage

Lord,
bless these your servants, _____ and _____,
who have been joined
in the holy covenant of matrimony
by a second nuptial veiling
in accordance with the Apostle's command.
May it have all the merit of a first marriage . . .

May they be worthy of the merits
of the patriarchal couples.
May peace, meekness,
and the gentleness of holiness be theirs.
Amen.

A Visigothic prayer; Spain, eleventh century

Prayer for the Sanctification of Holy Matrimony

O Eternal Light, into the dazzling darkness of Thine infinite presence we commend this man and this woman.

Let the holy fire of love burn through all barriers that might estrange them.

Grace them with that selflessness, that largeness of heart, through which _____ may become more truly himself and _____ more truly herself.

Over the washes of time's hurrying years, spread the wings of that eternity in which there is no shadow of turning.

And beneath the strife and tumult of this clamoring world, anchor them in that peace which the world can neither give nor take away, the peace that passes all understanding.
Amen.

Huston Smith; United States, twentieth century

LETTING EACH OTHER GO

For *this* is wrong, if anything is wrong:
not to enlarge the freedom of love
with all the inner freedom one can summon.
We need, in love, to practice only this:
letting each other go. For holding on
comes easily; we do not need to learn it.

Rainer Maria Rilke; Germany, 1875–1926,
translated by Stephen Mitchell

PRAYER FOR A FIANCÉE

That I may come near to her, draw me nearer to Thee than to her; that I may know her, make me to know Thee more than her; that I may love her with the perfect love of a perfectly whole heart, cause me to love Thee more than her and most of all. Amen. Amen.

That nothing may be between me and her, be Thou between us, every moment. That we may be constantly together, draw us into separate loneliness with Thyself. And when we meet breast to breast, my God, let it be on Thine own. Amen. Amen.

Temple Gairdner; England, 1873–1928

The Christian Marital Vows

Wilt thou, _____, have this woman to be thy wedded wife, to live together in the holy state of matrimony? Wilt thou love her, comfort her, honor and keep her, in sickness and in health; and forsaking all others keep only unto her, so long as ye both shall live?

I will.

And wilt thou, _____, have this man to be thy wedded husband, to live together in the holy state of matrimony? Wilt thou love him, comfort him, honor and keep him, in sickness and in health; and forsaking all others keep thee only unto him, so long as ye both shall live?

I will.

Repeat after me.

I, _____, take thee, _____, to be my wedded wife, to have and to hold, from this day forward, for better, for worse, for richer, for poorer, in sickness and in health, to love and to cherish, till death us do part, according to God's holy ordinance; and thereto I plight thee my troth.

I, _____, take thee, _____, to be my wedded husband, to have and to hold, from this day forward, for better, for worse, for richer, for poorer, in sickness and in health, to love and to cherish, till death us do part, according to God's holy ordinance; and thereto I plight thee my troth.

From the Order for the Solemnization of Matrimony; England, traditional

MARRIAGE: A BAHÁ'Í PRAYER

Glory be unto Thee, O my God! Verily this Thy servant and this, Thy maidservant, have gathered under the shadow of Thy mercy and they are united through Thy favor and generosity. O Lord! Assist them in this Thy world and Thy Kingdom and destine for them every good through Thy bounty and grace. O Lord! Confirm them in Thy servitude and assist them in Thy service. Suffer them to become the signs of Thy Name in Thy World and protect them through Thy bestowals, which are inexhaustible in this world and in the world to come. O Lord! They are supplicating the kingdom of Thy mercifulness and invoking the realm of Thy singleness. Verily they are married in obedience to Thy command. Cause them to become the signs of harmony and unity until the end of time.

Verily Thou art the Omnipotent, the Omnipresent, and the Almighty!

'Abdu'l-Bahá; Iran, 1844–1921

Since He Left Me

Unable to live since
he left me,
heart, body, breath given up—
night and day
a ghost on the highway
lured by the remembrance of beauty.
Lifting her throat,
Mira the slave girl cries out:
    Fetch me home!

Mirabai; India, 1498–1550, translated by
Andrew Schelling

HYMN TO LOVE

If I speak in the tongues of men and of angels, but have not love, I am nothing but a noisy gong or a clanging cymbal. And if I have the gift of prophecy, and understand all mysteries and knowledge, and if I have all faith, so as to move mountains, but have not love, I am nothing. If I give away all I have, and if I deliver my body to be burned, but have not love, I gain nothing at all.

Love is patient and kind; love is never jealous or boastful; it is not arrogant or rude. Love does not insist on its own way; it is not irritable or resentful; it does not rejoice at wrong, but rejoices in the right. Love bears all things, believes all things, hopes all things, endures all things.

Love never ends; as for prophecies, they will pass away; as for tongues, they will cease; as for knowledge, it will pass away. For our knowledge is imperfect, and our prophecy is imperfect. But when the perfect arrives, the imperfect will pass away. When I was a child, I spoke like a child, I thought like a child, I reasoned like a child; when I became a man, I gave up all childish ways. For now we see in a glass darkly, but then we will see face to face. Now I know only in part; then I will understand fully, even as I have been fully understood. In short, there are three things which last: faith, hope, and love, and the greatest of these is love.

1 Corinthians 13: 1–13

IF YOU HAVE LOST HEART

If you have lost heart
   on the path of love
Flee to Me without delay:
   for I am a fortress invincible.

Jalal-ud-Din Rumi; Persia,
1207–1273

THE QUEST FOR GOD

The whole history of humanity's tireless search for the Absolute, for the Infinite Source and Destiny of creation and the meaning of it all, is found in exquisite fullness in prayers of longing, prayers expressing the deepest, most elemental yearning of the mind and soul. All over the world, these most beautiful of prayers sound the depths of human experience, reaching all the way to the end of the heart's capacity for joy. Anselm of Canterbury wrote of his own quest for God, "I have known a joy that is full and more than full." Spiritual joy is a gift promised unconditionally at this stage of the sacred way.

This global treasury of prayers, surpassing the loveliest poetry, glowing in lyrical beauty and mystical ecstasy, emanates from a spirit held high to the Unnamable and saturated in grace. "You would not seek if you had not already found," wrote Pascal, honoring the simple, paradoxical truth that the Holy Presence exists within us and around us like the air we breathe, disclosing Itself equally to those who know they know God and to those as yet unconscious of Divine Reality. Whether one feels impassioned for the quest, or indifferent, whether one cares or not, God's radiance is always shimmering in oceans, intellects, skies, and eyes, as though life itself were a golden bowl filled with light.

137

Karl Rahner, the twentieth-century German theologian, presses against the limits of language when he tries to describe the Divine Object of his own contemplation:

> What shall I say to You, my God? Shall I collect together all the words which praise Your holy name, shall I give You all the names of this world, You, the Unnamable? Shall I call You God of my life, meaning of my existence, hallowing of my acts, my journey's end, bitterness of my bitter hours, home of my loneliness, You my most treasured happiness? Shall I say, Creator, Sustainer, Pardoner, Near One, Distant One, Incomprehensible One, God both of flowers and stars, God of the gentle wind and of terrible battles, Wisdom, Power, Loyalty, and Truthfulness, Eternity and Infinity, You the All-Merciful, You the Just One, You Love itself?

Here at the flaming ground of being, in this state of sacred freedom, where truth becomes obvious and rapturous, seekers like Rahner find consciously what they always possessed unconsciously, the vision of That Which Is, the Indefinable Reality that compels us to seek, nurtures the sacred quest, and receives us at its end.

WHAT SHALL I SAY TO YOU, MY GOD?

What shall I say to You, my God? Shall I collect together
all the words which praise Your Holy Name, shall I give You
all the names of this world, You, the Unnamable? Shall I call
You God of my life, meaning of my existence, hallowing of my
acts, my journey's end, bitterness of my bitter hours, home of
my loneliness, You, my most treasured happiness? Shall I say:
Creator, Sustainer, Pardoner, Near One, Distant One, Incomprehensible One, God both of flowers and stars, God of
the gentle wind and of terrible battles, Wisdom, Power, Loyalty, and Truthfulness, Eternity, and Infinity, You the All-
merciful, You the Just One, You, Love itself? . . .

What can I say to You, my God? Should I consecrate
myself to You? Should I say that I belong to You with all that
I have and am? O my God, how can I give myself to You,
unless Your grace accepts me? How can I devote myself to
Your service, unless You call me? I give You thanks for hav-
ing called me.

But what am I really saying, when I call You my God, the
God of my life? That you are the meaning of my life? The goal
of my wanderings? The consecration of my actions? The judgment of my sins? The bitterness of my bitter hours and my
most secret joy? My strength, which turns my own strength

into weakness? Creator, Sustainer, Pardoner, the One both far and near? Incomprehensible? God of my brethren? God of my fathers?

Are there any titles which I needn't give You? And when I have listed them all, what have I said? If I should take my stand on the shore of your Endlessness and shout into the trackless reaches of Your Being all the words I have ever learned in the poor prison of my little existence, what should I have said? I should have never spoken the last word about You.

Karl Rahner; Germany, 1904–1984

ALL MUST BE SET AT NAUGHT

The true seeker hunteth nought but the object of his quest, and the lover hath no desire save union with his beloved. Nor shall the seeker reach his goal unless he sacrifice all things. That is, whatever he hath seen and heard and understood, all must be set at naught, that he may enter the realm of the spirit, which is the City Of God. Labor is needed, if we are to seek Him; ardor is needed, if we are to drink of the honey of reunion with Him; and if we taste of this cup, we shall cast away the world.

Bahá'u'lláh; Iran, 1817–1892

THERE CAME TO YOUR STREET A GYPSY BEGGAR

There came to Your street a gypsy beggar
   hoping for a welcome
and fell, poor soul, in the dust at Your door.
   But he went nowhere, nowhere at all;
whom should he visit? where should he flee?
   with his leg snapped by the hand of desire?
He came to Your door, for in earth and heaven
   he found no place but there—
and how shall a beggar leave the gate
   of a King empty-handed?
Every second my eyes search Your face
   hungry for that blessed greeting
and from moment to moment my soul borrows
   subsistence from Your lips.
I searched here and there but found no corner
   to hide You in but my narrow heart.
Every face I see without Your face
   seems to me nothing but a beginning:
Wherever I tangled my heart in someone's
   tresses
     I gave myself to a dragon;

I drowned in my separation but no one,
  no friend took my hand.
In the world's mirror I beheld nothing
  but the world-displaying picture of Your face
for indeed all things of the world but You
  seem mere echo or mirage.
My eyes saw nothing, no purity
  in the darkness of the world;
I returned again to Your door
  hoping, praying for some hand-out.
In the garden of Your love, 'Iraqi
  is but a songless bird.

Fakhruddin 'Iraqi; Persia, c. 1213–c. 1289

Longing for You

O immeasurably tender love! Who would not be set afire with such love? What heart could keep from breaking? You, deep well of charity, it seems You are so madly in love with Your creatures that You could not live without us! Yet You are our God, and have no need of us. Your greatness is no greater for our well-being, nor are You harmed by any harm that comes to us, for You are supreme eternal Goodness. What could move You to such mercy? Neither duty nor any need you have of us (we are sinful and wicked debtors!) — but only love! . . .

O eternal God, light surpassing all other light because all light comes forth from You! O fire surpassing every fire because You alone are the fire that burns without consuming! You consume whatever sin and selfishness You find in the soul. Yet Your consuming does not distress the soul but fattens her with insatiable love, for though You satisfy her she is never sated but longs for You constantly. The more she desires You, the more she finds and enjoys You, high eternal fire, abyss of charity!

Catherine of Siena; Italy, 1347–1380

I Want Thee, Only Thee

That I want thee, only thee—let my heart repeat without end. All desires that distract me, day and night, are false and empty to the core.

As the night keeps hidden in its gloom the petition for light, even thus in the depth of my unconsciousness rings the cry—I want thee, only thee.

As the storm still seeks its end in peace when it strikes against peace with all its might, even thus my rebellion strikes against thy love and still its cry is—I want thee, only thee.

Rabindranath Tagore; India, 1861–1941

Thou Art the Luminous *Aum*

Thou art the luminous *Aum* and formless Being,
Affirmation and Negation art Thou too.
Thou art Certitude and Truth indeed art Thou,
The Essence of all living beings and Felicity art
  Thou.

Maha Yogi Siva Yogaswami; Sri Lanka,
1872–1964

Whither Shall I Go from Thy Spirit?

O Lord, thou hast searched me, and known me.
Thou knowest my downsitting and mine uprising,
Thou understandest my thought afar off.
Thou compassest my path and my lying down,
And art acquainted with all my ways.

For there is not a word in my tongue,
But, lo, O Lord, thou knowest it altogether.
Thou has beset me behind and before,
and laid thine hand upon me.
Such knowledge is too wonderful for me;
It is high, I cannot attain unto it.

Whither shall I go from thy spirit?
Or whither shall I flee from thy presence?
If I ascend up into heaven, thou art there:
If I make my bed in hell, behold, thou art there.

If I take the wings of the morning,
And dwell in the uttermost parts of the sea;
Even there shall thy hand lead me,
And thy right hand shall hold me.

If I say, Surely the darkness shall cover me;
Even the night shall be light about me.
Yea, the darkness hideth not from thee;
But the night shineth as the day:
The darkness and the light are both alike to thee . . .

How precious also are thy thoughts unto me, O God!
How great is the sum of them!
If I should count them, they are more in number than
    the sand:
When I awake, I am still with thee . . .

Search me, O God, and know my heart:
Try me, and know my thoughts:
And see if there be any wicked way in me,
And lead me in the way everlasting.

Psalm 139: 1–12, 17–18, 23–24

LIKE A WILD FLOWER

Lord, you are like a wild flower. You spring up in places where we least expect you. The bright color of your grace dazzles us. When we reach down to pluck you, hoping to possess you for our own, you blow away in the wind. And if we tried to destroy you, by stomping on you and kicking you, you would come back to life. Lord, may we come to expect you anywhere and everywhere. May we rejoice in your beauty. Far from trying to possess you, may you possess us. And may you forgive us for all the times when we have sinned against you.

Heinrich Suso; Germany, c. 1300–1366

AFTER CLIMBING MOUNT CARMEL

Mothlike You gnawed my desires my spirit is broken
My Lord, who leads me blind and enclosed through
   unfamiliar paths through unknown routes
Way, My God's ancient way, Jacob's ladder, Judith passes
   in the midst of enemies, disguised at night—they fail to
   recognize God's trail
You give me the spring of a doe and unto summits You
   prompt my steps
Give me a simple heart that fears Your Name
My soul rests in You like a child against its mother

Night when You create me anew You give me forgetfulness
   of my memory and my soul like a bird escaped from the
   nets of thought
I had eyes to see and did not see You
ears to hear and did not hear You
but I know that my eyes will see a land with broad
   expanses
they will contemplate Your Royal loveliness
Night—the phantasms, the mirages, and the dream of life
   have been dashed
Night which lightens my darkness

Night when You give birth to me Your chrysalis
Night when You guide me outside myself through a sure
    route
Night all distance abolished You give Yourself
You put Your desire in me and my womb trembles
at the touch of Your presence.
Your NAME

You beget it in an unknown virgin part of my being
and I become a reflection of Your face
beyond all knowing I only know Love

Lisa Boscane; France, twentieth century,
translated by Mary-Theresa McCarthy

LATE HAVE I LOVED THEE

Late have I loved Thee, O Beauty so ancient and so new; late have I loved Thee: for behold Thou wert within me, and I outside; and I sought Thee outside and in my unloveliness fell upon those lovely things that Thou has made. Thou wert with me, and I was not with Thee. I was kept from Thee by those things, yet had they not been in Thee, they would not have been at all. Thou didst call and cry to me to break open my deafness: and Thou didst send forth Thy beams and shine upon me and chase away my blindness: Thou didst breathe fragrance upon me, and I drew in my breath and do not pant for Thee: I tasted Thee, and now hunger and thirst for Thee: Thou didst touch me, and I have burned for Thy peace.

Saint Augustine; North Africa, 354–430

THOU ART HIDDEN FROM US

Thou art hidden from us, though the heavens are filled
With Thy Light, which is brighter than sun and moon!
Thou art hidden, yet revealest our hidden secrets!
Thou art the Source that causes our rivers to flow.
Thou art hidden in Thy essence, but seen by thy bounties.
Thou art like the water, and we like the millstone.
Thou art like the wind, and we like the dust;
The wind is unseen, but the dust is seen by all.
Thou art the Spring, and we the sweet green garden;
Spring is not seen, though its gifts are seen.
Thou art as the Soul, we as hand and foot;
Soul instructs hand and foot to hold and take.
Thou art as Reason, we like the tongue;
'Tis reason that teaches the tongue to speak.
Thou art as Joy, and we are laughing;
The laughter is the consequence of the joy.
Our every motion every moment testifies,
For it proves the presence of the Everlasting God.

Jalal-ud-Din Rumi; Persia, 1207–1273

Reveal Yourself

I no longer want just to hear about you, beloved Lord, through messengers. I no longer want to hear doctrines about you, nor to have my emotions stirred by people speaking of you. I yearn for your presence. These messengers simply frustrate and grieve me, because they remind me of how distant I am from you. They reopen wounds in my heart, and they seem to delay your coming to me. From this day onward please send me no more messengers, no more doctrines, because they cannot satisfy my overwhelming desire for you. I want to give myself completely to you. And I want you to give yourself completely to me. The love which you show in glimpses, reveal to me fully. The love which you convey through messengers, speak it to me directly. I sometimes think you are mocking me by hiding yourself from me. Come to me with the priceless jewel of your love.

Saint John of the Cross; Spain, 1542–1591

IN PRAISE OF AHURA MAZDA: A ZOROASTRIAN PRAYER

I address myself to Thee, Ahura Mazda, to Whom all worship is due. With outstretched arms and open mind and my whole heart, I greet Thee in spirit. Turn Thy countenance toward me, dear Lord, and make my face happy and radiant.

My heart yearns for Thee with a yearning which is never stilled. Thou art my most precious possession, greater and grander, lovelier and dearer by far than the life of my body and the life of my spirit. My joy is in Thee, my refuge is in Thee, my peace is in Thee. Let me live before Thee and with Thee and in Thy sight, I humbly pray.

From The Ahunovati Gatha; *Persia, c. 1200 B.C.E.*

When Will You Visit Me Again?

O everlasting Light, far surpassing all created things, send down the beams of Your brightness from above, and purify, gladden, and illuminate in me all the inward corners of my heart. Quicken my spirit with all its powers, that it may cleave fast and be joined to You in joyful gladness of spiritual rapture. Oh, when will that blessed hour come when You will visit me and gladden me with Your blessed presence, so that You are to me all in all? As long as that gift is not given me, there will be in me no full joy.

Thomas à Kempis; Germany, 1380–1471

Flood My Soul with Your Love

Lord Jesus Christ, flood my soul with your love so that I may always long for you alone, who are the bread of angels and the fulfillment of the soul's deepest desires. May my heart always hunger and feed upon you, so that my soul may be filled with the sweetness of your presence. May my soul thirst for you, who are the source of life, wisdom, knowledge, light, and all the riches of God our Father. May I always seek and find you, think upon you, speak to you, and do all things for the honor and glory of your holy name. Be always my only hope, my peace, my refuge, and my help in whom my heart is rooted so that I may never be separated from you.

Saint Bonaventure; Italy, 1221–1274

ARE YOU LOOKING FOR ME?

O dear friend
in search of
My Beloved,
I wandered
All over the earth
in far and distant lands;

But on meeting
With God,
My own courtyard
Became the universe!

Kabir; India, 1450–1518

To Whom Can We Turn?

Who, if I cried out, would hear me among angels'
hierarchies? and even if one of them pressed me
suddenly against his heart: I would be consumed
in that overwhelming existence. For beauty is nothing
but the beginning of terror, which we still are just able to
   endure,
and we are so awed because it serenely disdains
to annihilate us. Every angel is terrifying.
   And so I hold myself back and swallow the call-note
of my dark sobbing. Ah, whom can we ever turn to
in our need? Not angels, not humans,
and already the knowing animals are aware
that we are not really at home in
our interpreted world. Perhaps there remains for us
some tree on a hillside, which every day we can take
into our vision; there remains for us yesterday's street
and the loyalty of a habit so much at ease
when it stayed with us that it moved in and never left.
   Oh and night: there is night, when a wind full of infinite
   space
gnaws at our faces. Whom would it not remain for—that
   longed-after,

mildly disillusioning presence, which the solitary heart
so painfully meets? Is it any less difficult for lovers?
But they keep on using each other to hide their own fate.

Don't you know *yet?* Fling the emptiness out of your arms
into the spaces we breathe; perhaps the birds
will feel the expanded air with more passionate flying.

Rainer Maria Rilke; Germany, 1875–1926,
translated by Stephen Mitchell

I Am the Wind

I am the wind that breathes upon the sea,
I am the wave on the ocean,
I am the murmur of leaves rustling,
I am the rays of the sun,
I am the beam of the moon and stars,
I am the power of trees growing,
I am the bud breaking into blossom,
I am the movement of the salmon swimming,
I am the courage of the wild boar fighting,
I am the speed of the stag running,
I am the strength of the ox pulling the plough,
I am the size of the mighty oak tree,
And I am the thoughts of all people
Who praise my beauty and grace.

From The Black Book of Camarthan; *ancient Wales*

As the Waters of a River

I see you in all things, O my God. Infinity itself is your creation. And all around are the signs of your infinity: the bursting life of countless plants; the unending song of innumerable birds; the tireless movement of animals and insects. Nowhere can I see a beginning or an end of your creation.

I see the infinite beauty which infuses the entire universe. You are the king of the universe, and its beauty is your crown and scepter. I bow down in homage and adoration.

You are immortal, imperishable, the summit of all knowledge, the power behind all movement. You designed all things, and set them in motion.

The sun in your eye during the day, and the moon your eye at night. The wind is your breath, and the fertile brown earth is your heart.

By your power all things are created, and by your power they are destroyed. Birth and death are in your hands. I tremble with awe and wonder when I contemplate your power.

As the waters of a river flow to the sea, the path determined by the line of the valley, so we pass through life to death, our destiny mapped out by your will.

Lord, reveal yourself to me. Show me that love, not hatred, inspires your creation. Show me that mercy, not anger, guides my life. I do not ask to understand the mystery of your works; I only want to be assured of your goodness.

Arjuna, son of Padu; India, c. eighth century B.C.E.

Sivamayam

Look! everything is *Sivamayam.* Then who are you? Who am I? Who is your father? Who is your mother? Who are they, and what are all others? Are they all not *Sivam?* Are you still in doubt? Do you fear? Look! I in you and you in me, and all being ONE and One being all, remain changeless as ever before. Arise, know more and more.

All is well,
all is well,
all is well.

Maha Yogi Siva Yogaswami; Sri Lanka, 1872–1964

COMMITMENT TO THE WAY

nce the fire of desire for God has been kindled, longing for the illumined life is unquenchable. Occasionally a single event is so full of God that it awakens the slumbering imagination and stirs the deeper self from its rest in the underground chambers of the soul. Rabbi Abraham Joshua Heschel wrote of such powerful incidents:

> God is not always silent, and man is not always blind. In every life there are moments when there is a lifting of the veil at the horizon of the known, opening a sight of the eternal. Each of us has at least once in life experienced the momentous reality of God. Each of us has once caught a glimpse of the beauty, peace, and power that flow through the souls of those who are devoted to God. But such experiences are rare events. To some people they are like shooting stars, passing and unremembered. In others they kindle a light that is never quenched. The remembrance of that experience and the loyalty to the response of that moment are the forces that sustain our faith.

The revelation of God's presence blazing at the ground of the soul is like a great door opening on a vast land flooded with grace, offering endless possibilities for cultivation and flowering, for development of capacities asleep in the spiritual self. God's self-disclosure in such moments of grace inaugurates in those who pay attention an ardent lifelong work, for those who catch sight of Infinite Love will never abandon the quest for more and more. In a moment of sudden awakening, Catherine of Genoa prayed, "Can it be that Thou hast called me with such a great love, and made me to know in one instant that which words cannot express?" And when a Buddhist renunciant glimpsed the holy truth which the East calls "emptiness," he retired to a cave to meditate in solitude for twenty years.

Commitment to the spiritual life does not always begin with such abrupt explosions of grace. More frequently, the choice of devotion as a lifelong path spans years of painful oscillation between opposing ideals and contradictory attitudes. Materialism or simplicity? Doubt or faith? Community or solitude? Eventually we find a middle way, and the Divine grace and spiritual courage to choose that way, to "will one thing," as Kierkegaard said. In the discovery of this center and oneness and harmony, we are able to commend our souls to God and to the holy insecurity of traveling a path we can hardly see and will never understand—the most arduous path one can take in life, and the most glorious.

The passion for the Absolute, however aroused and however understood, brings about, almost imperceptibly, a shift in attitude, a shift from fruitless egocentricity to centeredness in

God. It is as though all one's former interests had slipped quietly to the periphery of the mind, and a powerful new vitality had begun to burn in the heart. Whatever depression, distress, or sadness went before—or returns in the future—is perceived from the new spiritual center as sacred, as part of the working out of God's will.

Climbing the Holy Mountain, leaving behind for good the flat fields of boring repetition, of buying and consuming, harming and being harmed, is a task not easily embraced. A Christian mystic wrote after years of wrestling with her own resistance:

O, my Lord, You were within my heart, and You asked of me only that I should return within, in order that I might feel Your presence. O, Infinite Goodness, You were so near, and I, running here and there to seek You, found You not!

Few people would set out on the mountainside, and fewer would stay with the sacred climb if they hadn't heard of faith like this, if they hadn't encountered love like this. The truth is that faith and love grow palpably with each curve of the road, with each surprise that the Divine Beloved sets in front of us. Commitment endures, faith perseveres, love lasts because a brilliant light shines in the cosmic night, and every dazzling glimpse of it promises more.

169

To Desire Nothing but God

Therefore
Let us desire nothing else
let us wish for nothing else
let nothing else please us
    and cause us delight
except our Creator and Redeemer and Savior,
the one true God,
Who is the Fullness of Good
    all good, every good, the true and supreme good
Who alone is Good
    merciful and gentle
    delectable and sweet
Who alone is holy
    just and true
    holy and right
Who alone is kind
    innocent
    pure
from Whom and through Whom and in Whom is
    all pardon
    all grace
    all glory

        of all the penitent and the just
        of all the blessed who rejoice together in heaven.
Therefore
let nothing hinder us
    nothing separate us
    or nothing come between us
Let all of us,
    wherever we are
    in every place
    at every hour
    at every time of day,
    every day and continually
believe truly and humbly
and keep in (our) heart
and love, honor, adore, serve
    praise and bless
    glorify and exalt
    magnify and give thanks to the
Creator of all
Savior of all who believe in Him
    and hope in Him
    and love Him
Who is
    without beginning and without end
    unchangeable, invisible,

indescribable, ineffable,
incomprehensible, unfathomable,
blessed, worthy of praise,
glorious, exalted on high, sublime,
most high, gentle, lovable,
delectable and totally desirable above all else
forever.
Amen.

Saint Francis of Assisi; Italy, 1182–1226

THE SMALLEST DOOR

Almighty Father, Son and Holy Ghost, eternal ever blessed
gracious God; to me the least of saints, to me allow that I may
keep a door in paradise. That I may keep even the smallest
door, the furthest, the darkest, coldest door, the door that is
least used, the stiffest door. If so it be but in Thine house, O
God, if so it be that I can see Thy glory even afar, and hear
Thy voice O God, and know that I am with Thee, Thee O
God.

Saint Columba; Ireland, 521–597

The Gayatri Mantra

O divine Beings of all three worlds, let us contemplate the glorious splendor of our Divine Creator, the Primal One, who, like the radiant sun, has the power to burn away all ignorance. May He grant us His grace and illumine our minds.

Rig Veda, *III, 62, 10; India, ancient oral tradition,* B.C.E.

A Cosmic Prayer for the Sacred Community

O Blessed One, eternal Source and Lord of creation, sustainer of all worlds, you embrace the whole cosmos within yourself, for everything exists in you. Let your cosmic winds come and breathe your everlasting Spirit on us. Let us inhale your divine Spirit and be inspired. Enlighten us in your truth. Pour your grace into our hearts. Wipe away our sin and all negativity. Transform us into your Love, and let us radiate that Love to all others. Inflame us with your unending life. Dissolve our limited way of being. And elevate us into your divine Life. Give us the capacity to share that Life with everyone. Shape us in your wisdom. Grant us your gentle and healing sensitivity toward all creatures. Give us your laughter and joy. Let us become that divine wisdom, sensitivity, laughter, and joy for all beings. We realize that we are members of that Sacred Community with all humankind, other species, Nature, and the entire cosmos. Grant us a heart that can embrace them all in you. Let us be in communion with you forever in the bliss of that Love: the love that Dante knew so well "moves the sun and other stars."

Brother Wayne Teasdale; United States, twentieth century

To Christ, Crucified

It is not the heaven
you have promised me, my Lord
that moves me to love you.

Nor is it the fear of hell
that bids me
give you no offense.

You move me, Lord; I am
moved on seeing you nailed
to a cross and mocked.

I am moved by the sight of your
tormented flesh; the insults you bore,
your bitter death, they move me.

Finally, it is your love that
moves me, and in such a way
that even if there were no heaven

I should love you
and if there were no hell
I should fear you.

You need not give me a reason
to love you, since even if I did
not hope for all that I hope for

in the same way which
I love you today,
I would love you still.

*Anonymous; Spain, Middle Ages,
translated by Thomas Feeny*

The Bodhisattva's Infinite Compassion

A Bodhisattva resolves: I take upon myself the burden of all suffering, I am resolved to do so, I will endure it. I do not turn or run away, do not tremble, am not terrified, nor afraid, do not turn back or despond.

And why? At all costs I must bear the burdens of all beings, in that I do not follow my own inclinations. I have made the vow to save all beings. All beings I must set free. The whole world of living beings I must rescue, from the terrors of birth, of old age, of sickness, of death and rebirth, of all kinds of moral offense, of all states of woe, of the whole cycle of birth-and-death, of the jungle of false views, of the loss of wholesome *dharmas*, of the concomitants of ignorance—from all these terrors I must rescue all beings . . .

Śikshāsamuccaya, 280 (Vajradhuaja Sūtra)

I Am Going into the Forest

O Lord,
be merciful.
For I am going into the forest.

Source unknown; European oral tradition

EVER DEEPER ROOTS IN LOVE

You, from whom we come
   And to whom we go,
   Unchanging love,
You give us time for change and growth
   In this time of great change in my life,
please, give me courage to change and grow
   and cheerfulness amidst growing-pain.
Let me take ever deeper roots in love
Make me faithful without clinging
And let me remain faithful in letting go.
Into your hands I lay my life
And the lives of all whom I love.
   Amen.

Brother David Steindl-Rast; United States,
twentieth century

LORD OF MY HEART

Lord of my heart, give me vision to inspire me, that, working or resting, I may always think of You.

Lord of my heart, give me light to guide me, that, at home or abroad, I may always walk in Your way.

Lord of my heart, give me wisdom to direct me, that, thinking or acting, I may always discern right from wrong.

Lord of my heart, give me courage to strengthen me, that, amongst friends or enemies, I may always proclaim Your justice.

Lord of my heart, give me trust to console me, that, hungry or well-fed, I may always rely on Your mercy.

Lord of my heart, save me from empty praise, that I may always boast of You.

Lord of my heart, save me from worldly wealth, that I may always look to the riches of heaven.

Lord of my heart, save me from military prowess, that I may always seek Your protection.

Lord of my heart, save me from vain knowledge, that I may always study Your Word . . .

Heart of my own heart, whatever may befall me, rule over my thoughts and feelings, my words and actions.

From The Black Book of Camarthan; *ancient Wales*

LOVE

Love bade me welcome; yet my soul drew back,
   Guilty of dust and sin.
But quick-ey'd Love, observing me grow slack
   From my first entrance in,
Drew nearer to me, sweetly questioning
   If I lack'd anything.

"A guest," I answer'd, "worthy to be here."
   Love said, "You shall be he."
"I the unkind, ungrateful? Ah, my Dear,
   I cannot look on Thee."
Love took my hand, and, smiling, did reply,
   "Who made the eyes but I?"

"Truth, Lord; but I have marr'd them; let me shame
   Go where it doth deserve."
"And know you not," says Love, "who bore the blame?"
   "My dear, then I will serve."
"You must sit down," says Love, "and taste My meat."
   So I did sit and eat.

George Herbert; England, 1593–1633

The One Thing Needful

Keep me from trying to do too much, O Lord my God, and from trying to do it all at once. I am overwhelmed by all my busyness and long for peace, for leisure, for deeper prayer. You know that all the things I do are good things, but too much of a good thing is no longer good. Help me remember that everything depends not on me but on you. The whole world, including my own little corner of the world, could get along well enough without me, but never for an instant without you. Why do I burden myself with all these unnecessary tasks, when only one thing is needful—to open my heart to your living word as I rest in your presence?

Curb my wild haste, O Lord, remind me to ease back. Help me change my ingrained habit of rushing, and my selfish habit of bypassing others in a mad dash for the finish that is just out of reach. I have hurt those who happen to be in the way when I am speeding along. I am sorry, God, for grieving these brothers and sisters who reflect your image. Teach me to take more time for people and to pace myself for a lifelong journey.

Help me to savor each minute of life that comes to me from your superabundant aliveness. Let me pause, without feeling guilty, to enjoy the flowers you have placed along my path— blossoms more beautiful than Solomon in all his glory—and to enjoy the bird songs and the sunsets. Permit me, Lord, to take the time to look lovingly upon the wonders of your creation, those splendid works of your hands that enfold me wherever I go. O Lord, my God, you are slowly guiding everything according to your eternal plan, and I surrender all my cares to your constant loving care for me. Amen.

Charles Cummings; United States, twentieth century

LORD OF THE UNIVERSE . . . IF YOU HAD CATTLE

Lord of the Universe!
It is apparent and known unto you,
that if you had cattle and gave them to me to tend,
though I take wages for tending from all others,
from you I would take nothing,
because I love you.

From the Sefer Hasidim; *Germany, twelfth to thirteenth century, translated by Olga Mark*

To Never Swerve

We pray to see the Truth that Love is God, that God is One and to behold the whole world as our kin. We pray to never swerve from the path of *Dharma* nor to ever disown our parent's guidance. Grant us . . . that whatsoever comes or goes we will not be affected or enticed by worldly gains. Grant us the will to ever serve in humility. Let us never forget the presence of our spiritual preceptor. O Lord, let us never violate the law of the land or waste our moments idly. May we ever cherish women. Help us to subdue our fear and anger and never be influenced by those with a lowminded nature. Let us never submit to false doctrines nor to ever speak ill of others. We pray for wisdom in pursuing our goals and to keep us above unrighteous acts. Help us to master our inner yoga and meditation that we may learn to restrain our anger and to keep our minds ever under control. May we ever do our work in earnest and never harbor ill-will. Inspire us to go far and wide to spread the noble truths of *dharma.* By Your grace may our spirits soar from earth to heaven in exaltation, rejoicing in the infinitude of Siva. May all our deeds be benevolent and untainted. May equity be our motto for all creeds. Let us chant with devotion that melts the heart, "Praise God, Praise God, Praise God," and learn to live in Your light forever.

Maha Yogi Siva Yogaswami; Sri Lanka, 1872–1964

My Lord and My God,
My Love and My All

Walking the dangerously thin line between complaint and lament, with the holy audacity of Saint Teresa, I say: "If this is the way You treat Your friends, no wonder You have so few!" But then, along with that wild woman of Ávila, I pray that since You have so few friends, we few had better be good ones! Make me one of Your *good* friends.

I am not who I was when You first called me in all my naïve enthusiasm. With wide-open eyes and a broken heart, I am far more sobered and yet more intoxicated than ever, more realistic and yet more romantic, more sorrowful and ever more joyous.

What an arduous business to balance all Your paradoxical demands on the tightrope of life: solitude and togetherness, fast and feast, love and detachment, work and prayer. I do not ask for a lightening of the burden, but only for greater strength to bear the weight, and greater wisdom to bear it creatively. Or, if it be Your will to have it crucify me, then grant me the grace to go gladly, not merely with resignation, but rollicking with laughter.

I wouldn't mind a cross of wood so much, but being nailed

to a desk and buried alive under mounds of paper and telephone calls is an ignominious way to go! But this is the way You have chosen for me. Do I need a better system or more surrender?

Your answer lies in the secret of Saint Ignatius: to work as though everything depends on me, and pray as though everything depends on You. I've pulled off one or the other over the years, but now I beg You to help me live out a better balance between the two. And if I can't, then burn my files or consume me with Your flames!

I am a bow in Your hands, Lord, and I am being overdrawn. Help me to discern when that overdrawing comes from my own drivenness and I need more stillness, more secretarial help, and time-management—and when that overdrawing is You and all I need is the willingness to say yes.

Whenever You move me into the public eye, strengthen Your interior hold on me. Keep me buried in the hiddenness of Your heart. As the demands of my life grow greater and my patience thins, help me to go the distance and live out my exile in this crucified paradise. And when I have given You my all, may I say, "I have only done my duty" (Luke 17:10).

Make me more Your fool, more Your spouse, more Your slave. Plunge me ever more deeply into a life of self-spending service, and despite my chronic weariness, let me never count the cost or measure the length of the arrow that pierces my heart. I am Your tragic-merry woman and lay down my life in union with You, my Suffering Servant, my Crucified Clown, My Bridegroom and my King.

Mother Tessa Bielecki; United States, twentieth century

THE PATH TO WISDOM

Every species of life has its own way of salvation,
They will not be antagonistic to one another.
If we leave our own path and seek for another way
Of salvation, we shall never find it.
If one wishes to find the true way
Right action will lead to it directly.
Who treads the Path in earnest
Sees not the mistakes of the world.
If we find fault with others,
We ourselves are also in the wrong.
When other people are in the wrong we should ignore it:
It is wrong to find fault with others . . .
This world is the Buddha-world
Within which enlightenment may be sought.
To seek enlightenment by separating from this world
Is as foolish as to search for a rabbit's horn.
Right views are called "transcendental,"
Erroneous views are called "worldly,"

But when all views, both right and erroneous, are
    discarded,
Then the essence of wisdom manifests itself.

From The Sutra of the Sixth Patriarch;
                                China, eighth century

GUIDE ME TO YOURSELF: A SUFI PRAYER

O my God, my unworthiness is clear enough to You. The state I'm in is not concealed from You. My request is that I might draw near to You, that I might have Your directive. Guide me then to Yourself by Your own light. Make me to stand in the truth of servanthood within Your hands.

My prayer to You is through the hiddenness of Your gentleness, the gentleness of Your way of dealing, through the very beauty of Your elusiveness, through the greatness of Your might and the utter secret of Your power, by all that is untold in Your transcendence.

I have taken Your Name for my citadel and pleaded the intercession of Your messenger Muhammad—the blessing and peace of God be upon him.

Ahmad al-Tijānī; Algeria, 1737–c. 1815

TO WILL ONE THING

FATHER IN HEAVEN! What is a man without Thee! What is all that he knows, vast accumulation though it be, but a chipped fragment if he does not know Thee! What is all his striving could it even encompass a world, but a half-finished work if he does not know Thee: Thee the One, who art one thing and who art all! So may Thou give to the intellect, wisdom to comprehend that one thing; to the heart, sincerity to receive this understanding; to the will, purity that wills only one thing. In prosperity may Thou grant perseverance to will one thing; amid distractions, collectedness to will one thing; in suffering, patience to will one thing. Oh, Thou that giveth both the beginning and the completion, may Thou early, at the dawn of day, give to the young man the resolution to will one thing. As the day wanes, may Thou give to the old man a renewed remembrance of his first resolution, that the first may be like the last, the last like the first, in possession of a life that has willed only one thing.

Søren Kierkegaard; Denmark, 1813–1855

I Do Not See the Road Ahead

MY LORD GOD, I have no idea where I am going. I do not see the road ahead of me. I cannot know for certain where it will end. Nor do I really know myself, and the fact that I think that I am following your will does not mean that I am actually doing so. But I believe that the desire to please you does in fact please you. And I hope I have that desire in all that I am doing. I hope that I will never do anything apart from that desire. And I know that if I do this you will lead me by the right road though I may know nothing about it. Therefore will I trust you always though I may seem to be lost and in the shadow of death. I will not fear, for you are ever with me, and you will never leave me to face my perils alone.

Thomas Merton; United States, twentieth century

Let Me Walk in Beauty

O GREAT SPIRIT

Whose voice speaks in the winds,
and in the trees
whose breath gives life to all the world.
Listen to Your creature!
Hear me!
I am small and weak.
I need Your power.
I need Your wisdom.
Let me walk in beauty,
 and let my eyes be glad
 beholding the red and golden dawn.
Make my hands touch all things
 You have made
 with love,
And help my ears to hear Your voice
 in everything.
Make me wise
that I may understand
the sacred teachings
you have taught;

Help me learn the lessons hidden
   in every leaf and every stone
   O *Wakan-Tanka,*
I need power
   not to be greater than my relations
   but to conquer the enemy in myself.
Make me ready to come to you always
   with a pure heart
   and with clear eyes,
So when the time comes for my life to fade away,
   as the sunset fades,
So may my spirit come to You
   with honor and without shame.

Adapted from a traditional Native American prayer

HEAVY WITH YOU

oh eternal beauty risen from the night
when the last dawn is dead, when the last star has sung its
last song, when the rose has smothered its fragrance—You
ARE
and now you have called me, I heard my name,
I knew it was mine.
peace immerses me like a river and sweeps me over
mountains.
I am heavy with you. Stars rise from the sea.
Lord, who comes to me to suffer flesh and suffer space and
    die time,
sap stretches roots in the vibration of waters. May
a pure language be given to me,
song from the
beginnings, infinity whose center is your gaze,
mildness of the hills, swell of the seas.

Lisa Boscane; France, twentieth century,
translated by Mary-Theresa McCarthy

You Continue to Call Me:
A Meditation on Luke 19:1–10

Gracious and loving God, you continue to call at our homes, school, and places of labor. Daily you pass under our sycamore tree, saying, "Come down, for today I must abide at your house." Like Zacchaeus, may we have the courage to journey with you into new hope and joyful service. May we come down from the safe places of ideology, theology, and academics. May we come down from the defensive notions of race, creed, color, gender, and class. May we come down from the dividing lines of denominations and sects. May we come down from the anguish and failures of the past. May we come down and live in the aliveness of possibility and not the despair of human liability. May we come down and no longer view our service to others from the safe distances of false human security. And when we have come down to walk with you and one another, grant us salvation in our serving, blessing in our generosity to others, and peace at the end of our journey. Shine the light of grace and forgiveness into the dark and unseen corners of our hearts. May we make room for you. May your spirit find in each of us a resting place. Amen.

Eugene Blair; United States, twentieth century

I Did Not Know It Would Be Today

I have always known
That at last I would
Take this road,
but yesterday
I did not know
it would be today.

Anonymous; Japan

FRAGMENT

As it was,
As it is,
As it shall be
Evermore,
O Thou Triune
Of grace!
With the ebb,
With the flow,
O Thou Triune
of grace!
With the ebb,
With the flow.

Celtic oral tradition; collected in Scotland,
nineteenth century

SUFFERING

When the skies have grown too dark and there is too much cold in the world, when soul-pain and physical pain have canceled out the joy of living, people of faith, whether they feel abandoned by God or not, turn toward the Blessed One for the only solace that never disappears. The Dinka people of the Sudan transmit from generation to generation the following prayer:

> *God has forsaken us*
> *The creator of the sun refuses us life.*
> *O cold-white moon,*
> *The creator of the sun refuses us life.*

Forsaken and desolate, they summon the strength to surrender, like Job, to the Power that makes the seas and the skies (Job 42:2–6). And their act of surrender, in the cold face of the harshest kind of reality, gives birth to a nobility of spirit little else on earth can equal.

The Bakongo natives of West Africa turn with similar forgiveness and humility to the very God who allows their suffering to go on and on. They pray:

Father, thy children are in great anguish.
Calm the tempest, for here live many of thy children.
Seest thou not that we are dying?

Far away, in the easternmost part of the world, separated by time as well as space, a Buddhist once wrote with the same accepting reverence, "Now that my house has been burned to the ground, I have an unobstructed view of the rising moon." Through the exalting and dignifying power received in the contemplative life, he could welcome even devastation as a gift.

On the other side of the world, Christian mystics and saints have also struggled to direct their own immense energies into the same holy attitude. Clare of Assisi, for example, in the following prayer, raised an anguished voice to the Absolute, not in a futile hope of freedom from suffering, but to experience her pain in the company of the Trusted One:

What shall we do?
Why do you forsake us in our misery,
or to whom do you leave us
who are so desolate?

No cynicism or self-pity contaminates her anguish; no denial or attempt to escape the aching darkness deadens her pain. Instead, she uses the words of a prayer to transmute incomprehensible suffering into an act of adoration, to rise above desolation on the wings of a spiritual will, a will purified of all egoistic striving, emptied of all self-centeredness.

God in privation. God in starvation. God in desperation. The prayers in this chapter show how people alive in the spirit in all eras of history and all parts of the world turn to God to endure the unendurable. And what they learn, what they are always trying to teach us, is that life's most intolerable, most unjust, most undeserved, inexplicable and cruel suffering becomes bearable when confronted in the void, not alone, but with God. And in the presence of the Beloved, one may even be able to discern within the mystery of pain a seed of immortality.

Passover, Bergen-Belsen, 1944

Our Father in heaven, behold it is evident and known to thee that it is our desire to do thy will and to celebrate the festival of Passover by eating matzah and by observing the prohibition of leavened food. But our heart is pained that the enslavement prevents us and we are in danger of our lives. Behold, we are prepared and ready to fulfill thy commandment: "And ye shall live by them and not die by them."

We pray to thee that thou mayest keep us alive and preserve us and redeem us speedily so that we may observe thy statutes and do thy will and serve thee with a perfect heart. Amen.

Anonymous Jewish prayer; written in Germany, twentieth century

FATHER, BEHOLD US, THE COLOMBIANS

Father, we are Colombians. In our country we now live through difficult, contradictory times. The huge majority of Colombians have been baptized in the name of the Blessed Trinity, and we call ourselves Christians. But there exists in our land a terrible state of violence: guerrilla attacks, frequently drug-related, institutional violence, assassinations, paramilitary groups, robbers, common felons.

Father, man's most sinister behavior is that of Cain, who killed his brother, and that of Judas, who betrayed his own Master.

We know that throughout history mankind has been plagued by treachery and murder, but today we suffer from both with great frequency and terror. A price is put on a life, and for money—much or little—brother hunts brother and kills him, as did Cain.

At times one asks, just as Judas did, "How much will you give me if I hand them over to you? How much is it worth to you to be rid of So-and-so?" "How much is your country worth? How much will you advance me?"

Father, failure to see You as our common father is what most hardens our heart, changing us from brothers to enemies.

We would like to meet for a month and together cry out to You, Father, our Father, that we might realize we are brothers.

Father, we want to experience and to sow in our hearts the conviction that if each of us changes, a small part of Colombia will change.

Father, You are love and Your love is sown in the heart of everyone. May Your goodness take us by the hand and lead us from the slaughterhouse in which we live.

Father, we have faith that You gaze on us with all the force of Your saving love and all the kindness and comprehension of Your mercy.

José Mira; Colombia, twentieth century, translated by Thomas Feeny

GOD HAS FORSAKEN US

God has forsaken us,
The Creator of the sun refuses us life.
O cold white moon,
The Creator of the sun refuses us life.

Sudan; oral tradition

A MUSLIM PRAYER OF REPENTANCE

O God, I seek refuge with Thee, lest I be like a servant who repented before Thee unworthily, though he had knowledge of Thy mysteries, and returned back to his transgression and his sin. Make this my penitence such that I do not need after it yet another penitence, again to put away its sequel and to abide securely.

O my God, I acknowledge my ignorance before Thee and have nought but my ill-doing wherewith to come before Thee. In Thy patience take me into the shelter of Thy mercy and hide me graciously in the curtain of Thy pardon.

O my God, I repent before Thee of all that is in the thoughts of my heart, sight of my eyes, the words of my tongue, that contravenes Thy will or falls away from Thy love . . .

O God, have mercy upon me, lonely as I am. Under Thy hand and in awe of Thee, my heart is anguished and for very fear of Thee my frame is troubled. My transgressions, O God, have brought me near to requital in the loss of Thee. Were I to keep silent none would speak for me and were I to try to intercede I have no leave or means . . .

Spread Thy mercy to take me wholly in and hide me in the glory of Thy veil. Do with me as greatness would with a worthless servant who cried and was granted mercy or as one rich in wealth who heard a poor man's plea and refreshed him. For, O my God, I have no defender from Thee: let Thy might be my defense and let Thy goodness be my intercessor. My sins have made me afraid: Let Thy pardon set me at rest.

Attributed to Ali, son-in-law of Muhammad; Arabia, seventh century

A Sixteen-Year-Old Gangster's Prayer

Heavenly Father, please hear me
   tonight.
I need so much guidance to live my life
   right,
Sometimes the pressure is so hard to bear,
I often wonder if anyone cares.

How can I wake up and face a new day
Knowing I have to live my life in this
   crazy way?
Heavenly Father, forgive all my sins,
I want to change, but where do I begin?

Please God, bless my family, whose eyes
   silently plead
For me not to go out, as they all watch me
   leave.
And God bless my mother, who cries every
   night,
Worrying I'll be killed in another gun
   fight.

Heavenly Father, please answer my
   prayer

Please let me know you're listening up
   there.
When will it end? What's it all for?
To prove to my homies I'm down, I'm
   hardcore?

Sometimes I even wonder how I will die,
By a bullet wound or a knife in my side?
Heavenly Father, please hear me
   tonight,
Give me courage and strength to live my
   life right.

Please show me the way, Lord, show me
   the light.
Help change my heart so I won't have to
   fight.
Thank you for forgiveness, Lord, and for
   still being there.
Most of all, thank you for listening to
   this sinner's prayer. Amen.

Anonymous sixteen-year-old boy; United States,
twentieth century

ALL IS GONE

Father have pity on me,
Father have pity on me;
I am crying for thirst,
I am crying for thirst;
All is gone — I have nothing to eat,
All is gone — I have nothing to eat.

*Arapaho ghost dance song; Native
America, oral tradition*

A Jain Prayer for Forgiveness

For violence I have committed mentally,
For violence I have committed verbally,
For violence I have committed physically,
I ask forgiveness.

Ancient Jain tradition; India

I Was Hungry

Lord, when did we see you hungry?

I was hungry and you were flying around the moon.
I was hungry and you told me to wait.
I was hungry and you formed a committee.
I was hungry and you talked about other things.

I was hungry
    and you told me: "There is no reason."
I was hungry
    and you had bills to pay for weapons.
I was hungry and you told me:
    "Now machines do that kind of work."

I was hungry and you said:
    "Law and order come first."
I was hungry and you said:
    "There are always poor people."
I was hungry and you said:
    "My ancestors were hungry too."
I was hungry and you said:
    "After age fifty, no one will hire you."

I was hungry and you said:
   "God helps those in need."
I was hungry and you said:
   "Sorry, stop by again tomorrow."

Anonymous Lutheran prayer; twentieth-century France,
translated by Mary-Theresa McCarthy

A Prayer to the Divine Mother

O Divine Mother,
In this extreme danger,
when we and all sentient beings
and nature itself,
    herself,
    Your glorious body,
face unprecedented misery and destruction,
inaugurate in fierceness and in tenderness
the splendor of
    Your Age of Passionate Enlightenment.
Bring us into the fire of Your sacred passion for reality,
rejoin the severed mandala of our being,
infuse our bodies, our hearts, our souls, our minds,
with the calm and focused ecstasy of Your highest
    illumination
that brings each of those things into mutual harmony.
Engender in the ground of all our beings
the sacred marriage,
that union between masculine and feminine
from which in each of us the Divine Child is born,
    that Child that is flesh of Your flesh,
        heart of Your heart,
        light of Your light,

that Child that is free from all dogma,
    free from all shame,
    free from all false divisions
        between holy and unholy
        sacred and profane,
    free to burn out in love,
    free to play in love,
    free to serve in love,
        as love
        for love
in the heart of Your burning ground of life.
And teach us, O Divine Mother,
at every moment in this hour of apocalypse
the appropriate action that heals
    and preserves
    and redeems
    and transforms.

Andrew Harvey; United States, twentieth century,
dedicated to Rose Solari

DARKNESS SONG

We wait in the darkness!
Come, all ye who listen,
Help in our night journey;
Now no sun is shining;
Now no star is glowing;
Come, show us the pathway.
The night is not friendly;
It closes its eyelids;
The moon has forgotten us;
We wait in darkness!

Native America; Iroquois oral
tradition

A FATHER'S PRAYER UPON THE MURDER OF HIS SON: MAY 6, 1980

O God
We remember not only our son but also his murderers;
Not because they killed him in the prime of his youth and
   made our hearts bleed and our tears flow,
Not because with this savage act they have brought further
   disgrace on the name of our country among the civilized
   nations of the world;
But because through their crime we now follow thy
   footsteps more closely in the way of sacrifice.
The terrible fire of this calamity burns up all selfishness and
   possessiveness in us;
Its flame reveals the depth of depravity and meanness and
   suspicion, the dimension of hatred and the measure of
   sinfulness in human nature;
It makes obvious as never before our need to trust in God's
   love as shown in the cross of Jesus and His
   Resurrection;
Love which makes us free from hate toward our
   persecutors;
Love which brings patience, forbearance, courage, loyalty,
   humility, generosity, greatness of heart;

Love which more than ever deepens our trust in God's final
   victory and His eternal designs for the Church and for
   the world;
Love which teaches us how to prepare ourselves to face our
   own day of death.
O God
Our son's blood has multiplied the fruit of the Spirit in the
   soil of our souls;
So when his murderers stand before thee on the day of
   judgment
Remember the fruit of the Spirit by which they have
   enriched our lives.
And forgive.

Bishop Hassan Dehqani-Tafti; Iran, twentieth century

Prayer of a Chaplain on the Way to Jail

Compassionate God (who spent some time as a prisoner Yourself), You promised that we could meet You in the suffering of our sisters and brothers: "When I was in prison, You visited me" (Matthew 25). Let me meet You there today.

Teresa—a "drug mule" and an inconsolable Rachel, weeping for her children—the Body of Christ.

John—struggling to forgive himself for killing a little boy while driving during an alcoholic blackout—the Body of Christ.

Tom—resisting bitterness with hope and humor, although convicted of murdering his girlfriend despite evidence to the contrary—the Body of Christ.

Steven—grateful for this second chance and for each breath of life, certain that if he were not in jail, he would be dead or responsible for someone else's death—the Body of Christ.

José—at nineteen, the father of seven, who does not promise to stop selling guns and drugs to support his family when he returns to the streets—the Body of Christ.

Martha—alone, now that her husband, children, and parents, in exhaustion and disappointment, have left her to work out her own future—the Body of Christ.

Matthew—leaving this message for his brothers on the day of his release: "This is a House of Pain, but here I discovered the essential truth for my life: I am never alone," and posing this question to us all: "Why do we have to hide the sins and mistakes which are so important to the person we are becoming?"—the Body of Christ.

Ground me in hope. Open my eyes and my ears so that I can catch the coming of Your kingdom in our midst. Remind me that we are one in sin and one in grace.

"Remember those who are in prison, for you are prisoners with them yourselves" (Hebrews 13). Who was it who wrote, "Don't say, 'There but for the grace of God go I.' Say 'There go I.'" Indeed, we are all doing our own time in our own jails. Fear? Greed? Envy? Racism? Anger? Addiction?

Give us this day Your own holy passion for our freedom, so that we will obey the words You spoke to those watching Lazarus come forth: "Unbind him and let him go!" (John 11) Amen.

Lorette Piper; United States, twentieth century

THE TREE HAS NEVER BLOOMED

With tears running, O Great Spirit,
Great Spirit, my Grandfather
—with running tears I must say now
that the tree has never bloomed.
You see me here, an old man. Here at the
    center
of the world, where you took me
when I was young and taught me;
here, old, I stand,
and the tree is withered,
Grandfather, my Grandfather!

Again,
and maybe the last time on this earth,
I recall the great vision you sent me.
It may be
that some little root of the sacred tree still lives.
Nourish it then,
that it may leaf and bloom and fill with singing
    birds.
Hear me, not for myself, but for my people;
I am old. Hear me

that they may once more go back into the
   sacred hoop
and find the good red road,
the shielding tree!

Black Elk; Native America, Oglala Sioux tradition

PSALM OF A TORTURE VICTIM

I will praise You, Lord, for my joy!
I will sing to You and proclaim Your wonders!
At the time of persecution,
when I was imprisoned for defending the oppressed,
delivered to the soldier-hearted enemy of the people,
exposed like all captives
to insults and torture,
You, Lord, were listening to my plea.
You were participating in my defense.
You were giving me strength in adversity
and courage to face the assaults of cowards
who put their trust in the design
and might of their arms.
But *You* are mightier than armies,
with their helicopters and their grenades.
Their power will not endure
without the support of Your people.
You, Lord, who are freedom,

You who are hope for the vulnerable,
You who are mighty, I will sing to You:
endlessly will I proclaim Your name.

*Anonymous; Central America, twentieth century,
translated by Mary-Theresa McCarthy*

To Tlaloc, for Rain

O most human Lord and generous giver, sovereign of all things green and of the grain, Lord of the earthly paradise, Lord of incense.

Great is our sorrow, Lord, to see the whole earth parched with thirst, unable to create, unable to produce grain and trees and anything to sustain us. As a father and a mother, it conceived us and suckled us with the grain and fruit it bore: and now all is burned, all is lost, nothing reappears, inasmuch as the Gods of Tlaloque have borne everything away with them and concealed it in their hiding places, in their dwelling which is the earthly paradise. O most merciful Lord, Ruler of all things green and of rubber, and of fragrant and medicinal herbs, we implore thee to look with a benign eye upon the people of thy race, of thy reign, of thy possessions, who are now spent, lost, in peril, and dying. All things are perishing, and even the beasts and the animals and the birds die and fall without any cure.

Succor the God of the Earth, O Lord, with a little rain, for he conceives and sustains us when there is water. Grant, O Lord, to the people to receive this boon and this favor from thy hand. Grant that the people deserve to see and rejoice in green things and plants which are like precious stones and fruit and the sustenance of the Tlaloques. Let the dry clouds carry the rain and scatter it over us. Deign, O Lord, to grant that animals and plants be merry and rejoice; grant that the birds and the precious feathered flyers, like the quechol and the zacuan, soar and sing and taste green buds again.

With a great sighing and anguish of heart, I call upon and invoke all ye that are Gods of Water, ye that sleep in the four corners of the world, in the east, in the west, to the south, and to the north, ye that dwell in the cavities of the earth or in the deep caverns, so that ye may come and console this poor people, and water the earth, so that the eyes of the inhabitants of the earth, men, beasts, and birds, may, with renewed hope, praise your persons.

O Lords, deign to come!

Mexico; oral tradition

233

Renewal of Strength: A Meditation on Isaiah 40:27–31 and Matthew 5:1–12

When I woke up this morning, Lord, the day was already spent. Before I placed my feet on the floor, I was exhausted. I had laundry to do, groceries to buy, kids to deliver and pick up, bills to pay, problems to confront, and friends to console. I seem to never catch up, never see the end, and never find relief. Amidst the push and pull of everyday living, I have no time for me. I have no time for You. The center of my life, that place where I am to dwell in communion with You, is vacant and empty. I am on the edge and Your light is far from me. I am tired, I am weary, I am faint, and I am weak. I cannot remember the last time I prayed, spent sacred moments in silence, or read with a contemplative spirit Your Holy Word. Though I once soared like an eagle, high above any brokenness or despair of spirit, my wings are now clipped and sit mired in the clay of pity and hopelessness. Remind me, again, Great God, that You know no weariness, that You know no despair. Create in me a new spirit, Search me and understand me. Help me to receive Your power and strength in this great hour of need. Bless me, for I am poor in spirit. Bless me, for I mourn. Bless me, for I am persecuted. I am waiting on You and You alone to renew my strength that I might mount up once again like an eagle. May I run and not get weary. May I walk and not faint. May I know once again that You are God. Amen.

Eugene Blair; United States, twentieth century

PRAYER OF A HUNGRY MAN

God of our fathers, I lie down without food,
I lie down hungry,
Although others have eaten and lie down full.
Even if it be but a polecat, or a little rock-rabbit,
Give me and I shall be grateful!
I cry to God, Father of my ancestors.

South Africa; oral tradition

A PRAYER FOR TRUE UNDERSTANDING

O God
Give me understanding
Teach me patience and acceptance.

Whatever happened in the past, happened for the best.
Whatever is happening now, is also happening for the best.

I came with nothing and I will leave with nothing.
What belonged to someone else yesterday is mine today,
What is mine today will belong to someone else tomorrow.

In this ever-changing world
Is an unchanging principle
Which is within my own being.

Contentment and freedom arise from true understanding
The Self is one and the same in all.

Swami Nitayananda; India, twentieth century

WHY HAVE YOU ABANDONED ME?

My God, my God, why have You abandoned me?
I am a human caricature, scorned by people.
All the newspapers ridicule me.
Armored tanks surround me,
machine guns point at me,
barbed wire encircles me, electrified barbed wire.
They stripped me of all identity,
they led me naked to the gas chamber,
they divided my clothes among them, and my shoes.

But I will be able to tell others about You,
I will exalt You in the assembly of our people,
my hymns will resound in the heart of a great people.
The needy will have a banquet,
our people will celebrate a magnificent festival—
the revolutionary people ready to emerge.

Ernesto Cardenal; Nicaragua, 1925,
translated by Mary-Theresa McCarthy

JOB'S DESPAIR

Why did I not die at birth,
   come forth from the womb and expire?
Why did the knees receive me?
   Or why the breasts, that I should suck?
For then I should have lain down and been quiet;
   I should have slept; then I should have been at rest,
with kings and counsellors of the earth
   who rebuilt ruins for themselves,
or with princes who had gold,
   who filled their houses with silver.
Or why was I not as a hidden untimely birth,
   as infants that never see the light?
There the wicked cease from troubling,
   and there the weary are at rest . . .

Why is light given to him that is in misery,
   and life to the bitter in soul,
who long for death, but it comes not,
   and dig for it more than for hid treasures;
who rejoice exceedingly,
   and are glad, when they find the grave?
Why is light given to a man whose way is hid,
   whom God has hedged in?

For my sighing comes as my bread,
and my groanings are poured out like water.
For the thing that I fear comes upon me,
and what I dread befalls me.
I am not at ease, nor am I quiet;
I have no rest; but trouble comes.

Job 3:11–17, 20–26

IF YOUR BODY DOES NOT
RESEMBLE MINE

Lord, under shellfire my body blew
    apart.
Bombs dismembered it.
All that remains of it is debris
scattered in the streets,
suspended from balconies
with my blood sticking
beneath the feet of passersby.
Lord,
if Your body does not resemble
    mine,
with all its strewn pieces,
how can I tell You:
Have pity on me!

Glory to You, Lord,
whose death was happy:
You kept Your body on the cross,
You kept Your body in the tomb.
Lord,

they divided Your mantle:
but it is my body
that was divided . . .
And my pain has been sown
to the ends of the earth,
and my cry has been heard
along every path.
Lord, reassemble my body!

And since You are the Resurrection,
since our existence wends its way
toward You,
since You have found nothing
more pure than my body
to sow joy, love, and peace
in the heart of the earth,
I say to You, Lord:
Sow, sow my body
in a land of love.
May springtime come to life
out of my pain.
May my body stand before You
like a flame,
may Your body be glorified
in my martyrdom,

may I be able to say
in a cry of joy:
Alleluia! Glory to You, Lord!

*Anonymous; Vietnam, twentieth century,
translated by Mary-Theresa McCarthy*

Kwambaza: A Cry for Help

O Imana (God) of Urundi (Ruanda), if only you would
  help me!
O Imana of pity, Imana of my father's home (country), if
  only you would help me!
O Imana of the country of the Hutu and the Tutsi, if only
  you would help me just this once!
O Imana, if only you would give me a homestead and
  children!
I prostrate myself before you, Imana of Urundi.
I cry to you: Give me offspring, give me as you give to
  others!
Imana, what shall I do, where shall I go?
I am in distress; where is there room for me?
O Merciful, O Imana of mercy, help me this once!

Sudan; oral tradition

HEAL MY BROKENNESS

O my God, only Your kindness and compassion can heal my brokenness. My poverty nothing can enrich but Your gentleness and goodness. Only grace from You can calm my agitation. My frailty Your power alone can strengthen. My longings nothing but Your bounty will ever satisfy. My destitution will be made good by Your wealth alone. My need of You none other can fulfil. Only Your mercy can gladden my distress. My sorrow of heart only Your compassion will relieve. My thirst will not be slaked unless You reach to me, nor my fearing soul be set at rest except I find You.

Only the sight of Your countenance of grace can meet my deepest yearning. It is only in drawing near to You that rest is truly mine. Your Spirit only will restore my broken heart: my sickness only Your medicine will heal. It is only when You are near that my grief is lifted. Only Your pardon laves my wound. The stain in my heart only Your forgiveness can take away. It is Your command alone that stills the whispering in my bosom.

For You are the utmost hope of the hopeful, the goal of the quest of the questioners, the ultimate that petitioners seek, the crown of all that men desire. You are the guardian of the well-doers, the security of the timorous, the treasure of the deprived, the wealth of the destitute, the succor of those who cry for help, the satisfier of the needs of the poor and the wretched. On You I call, O most merciful and gracious. I humble myself before You and make my plea. My cry and my yearning are that You would refresh me with Your kindly Spirit and continue to me Your good pleasure.

For here I am standing at the door of Your goodness, setting myself in the way of Your righteousness to breathe upon me, and taking firm hold of the strong rope — the sure grasp of one who clings to You. O my God, do mercy to Your unworthy servant, whose word is faint, whose deed is scant. In Your rich forbearance do well to him. Shelter him under Your shade, You who are Lord of all the merciful, kingly, glorious, and mighty.

Munājāt Zain al-'Ábidìn; Iran, twelfth to thirteenth century

MERGER: A VISION OF THE FUTURE

And then all that has divided us will merge
And then compassion will be wedded to power
And then softness will come to a world
that is harsh and unkind
And then both men and women will be gentle
And then both women and men will be strong
And then no person
will be subject to another's will
And then all will be rich and free and varied
And then the greed of some
will give way to the needs of many
And then all will share equally
in the earth's abundance
And then all will care
for the sick and the weak and the old
And then all will nourish the young
And then all will cherish life's creatures
And then all will live
in harmony with each other and the earth.
And then everywhere
will be called Eden once again.

Judy Chicago; United States, twentieth century

ARRIVING AT ELDERHOOD

The spiritual task of elderhood is wisdom. The time has arrived for gathering gifts that could not be harvested earlier, for integrating everything that went before, the memories and realities of each decade gone by, all the good and bad, what was wanted and unwanted, sought and unsought. The moment dawns for contemplating one's place in the long context of unfolding history, for contemplating the magnificent dynamism in the cosmos, how everything moves together in one ecstatic, exquisite dance, how the entire universe suffers when the tiniest firefly is hurt. This deep contemplation, a most sacred gift, like the blessings of time and solitude, leads to greater and greater understanding, and pours such a shower of grace on the inner seed of wisdom that, after a lifetime of slow growth, it bursts into full flowering. Understanding is the beginning of wisdom; wisdom begins Eternal Life.

Because elderhood so vastly widens spiritual vision, because elders have been on earth long enough "to learn to bear the beams of love," as Blake once said, old men and women experience an enlarged capacity for God. Closer in time to the Infinite, quietly nearing eternity with each passing day, drawing farther and farther away from the merely material world, the old see persons, things, events in the context of God, and comprehend what could not possibly be comprehended earlier. What made no sense without God, makes every sense with God—as the writer of the Psalms knew so well:

Then thought I to understand this,
but it seemed to me a wearisome task,
until I went into the sanctuary of God (Psalm 73:16–17).

In Wisdom Literature, scriptures, and prayers throughout the world, elderhood is like a golden age, a paradise peopled with spiritual heroes and heroines, who have matured like the fruit of the vine, have ripened, have touched the tree of wisdom with their own hands, and at last know happiness (Proverbs 3:18). The human spirit can now soar to the heights of the Holy Mountain, and breathe deeply in the airy freedom and spaciousness found only there. Spiritual courage can overcome physical diminishments, all feelings of fear give way to holy acceptance, while the heart prepares for separation.

The most sacred gift of elderhood, the beginning of the real, uncovered, everlasting vision of God—of the full blazing glory of God—which in its totality is withheld for eternity, is like the moment just before the parting of the veil. Rainer Maria Rilke, who understood this, wrote:

Nearing death one doesn't see death, but stares beyond, perhaps with an animal's vast gaze. Lovers, if the beloved were not there blocking the view, are close to it, and marvel . . . As if by some mistake, it opens for them behind each other. (Translated by Stephen Mitchell)

Lovers "are close to it"; the elderly arrive. With eyes like spotless windows overlooking the fields of eternity, those closest to death are granted life's greatest opportunity to view, to behold, to gaze on the luminous horizon stretching out before us all. Infused with a special grace not granted to the young, the old are ready to absorb the Light they see and, like mirrors, reflect it to those not yet pure enough, mature enough, transparent enough to image such holiness. "The heavenly person in whom God shines," to borrow Meister Eckhart's words, becomes in the last decades of life capable of serenely illumining the world with Living Light.

THOU HAST MADE ME ENDLESS

Thou hast made me endless, such is thy pleasure. This frail vessel thou emptiest again and again, and fillest it ever with fresh life.

This little flute of a reed thou has carried over hills and dales, and hast breathed through it melodies eternally new.

At the immortal touch of thy hands my little heart loses its limits in joy and gives birth to utterance ineffable.

Thy infinite gifts come to me only on these very small hands of mine. Ages pass, and still thou pourest, and still there is room to fill.

Rabindranath Tagore; India, 1861–1941

TO LORD KRISHNA

Every thought of my mind,
every emotion of my heart,
every movement of my being,
every feeling and every sensation,
each cell of my body, each drop of my blood
—all, all is yours,
yours absolutely,
yours without reserve
you can decide
my life or my death, my happiness or my sorrow,
my pleasure or my pain.
Whatever you do with me,
whatever comes to me from you,
will lead me to the Divine Rapture.

Bhāgavata Purāna; *India,*
ancient Vaishnava Hindu oral tradition,
recorded c. 800

DEEP PEACE

Deep peace of the running wave to you,
Deep peace of the flowing air to you,
Deep peace of the quiet earth to you,
Deep peace of the shining stars to you,
Deep peace of the Son of Peace to you.
Amen.

*Celtic oral tradition; Britain, Ireland,
Scotland, Wales, first millennium* C.E.

REMAIN WITH US

Remain with us, Lord
for evening approaches
and daylight dwindles.
Remain with us
and with your entire Church.
Remain with us
as daylight dwindles,
as our lives dwindle,
at the end of the world.

Remain with us,
through your grace and kindness,
through your sacred Word and
    sacrament,
through your help and benediction.

Remain with us
when we are visited
by nighttime's torment and anguish,
nighttime's doubts and temptations,
the painful nighttime of death.

Remain with us and all the faithful
world without end.
Amen.

*Wilhelm Löhe; Bavaria (Germany),
1808–1872, translated by Mary-
Theresa McCarthy*

EVENING PRAYER

Now that evening has fallen,
To God, the Creator, I will turn in prayer,
Knowing that he will help me.
I know the Father will help me.

Sudan; Dinka oral tradition

PSALM OF THE SISTERS

Though I be suffering and weak, and all
My youthful spring be gone, yet have I come
Leaning upon my staff, and clambered up
The mountain peak.
                My cloak thrown off,
My little bowl o'erturned, so sit I here
Upon the rock. And o'er my spirit sweeps
The breath of liberty! 'Tis won, 'tis won,
The Triple Lore!
The Buddha's will is done!

*Theragāthā, Psalm 24, Pāli canon; Theravada
Buddhist oral tradition, sixth to third century*
B.C.E.

Prayer of Surrender

O my Father, I surrender my whole self to you.
Do with me as you please! Whatever you do, I will thank
   you for it.
I am ready for anything, ready to accept whatever comes.
As long as your will is accomplished in me and within all
   creation,
   I ask for nothing else.
Into your hands I hand over my life.
To you I give it, my God, with all my heart's love.
I love you, and so I feel compelled to do as lovers do—to
   give
myself, to put myself entirely in your hands, with infinite
   trust,
for I know you are my Father! Amen.

Charles de Foucauld; France, 1838–1916,
translated by Charles Cummings

THE ROAD TO COLD MOUNTAIN

I climb the road to Cold Mountain,
The road to Cold Mountain that never ends.
The valleys are long and strewn with stones;
The streams broad and banked with thick grass.
Moss is slippery, though no rain has fallen;
Pines sigh, but it isn't the wind.
Who can break from the snare of the world
And sit with me among the white clouds?

Han-Shan; China, c. seventh to eighth century

A Sunny Dawn

My night has become a sunny dawn because of Your face,
  even though dusk has come to the sky.
Many are they who remain in the darkness of their night,
  while we are in the dazzling brilliance of Your face.

Ibn 'Abbad of Ronda; Spain, 1332–1390

The Sweet Uses of Adversity

O blessed pain and sickness and fever! O welcome weariness and sleeplessness by night! Lo! God of His bounty and favor Has sent me this pain and sickness in my old age; He has given me pain in the back, that I may not fail To spring up out of my sleep at midnight; That I may not sleep all night like the cattle, God in His mercy has sent me these pains. At my broken state the pity of kings has boiled up, And hell is put to silence by their threats!

Pain is a treasure, for it contains mercies; The kernel is soft when the rind is scraped off. O brother, the place of darkness and cold Is the fountain of life and the cup of ecstasy. So also is endurance of pain and sickness and disease. For from abasement proceeds exaltation. The spring seasons are hidden in the autumns, And autumns are charged with springs; flee them not. Consort with grief and put up with sadness, Seek long life in your own death!

Jalal-ud-Din Rumi; Persia, 1207–1273

THE HOLY ONE DISGUISED

The Holy One disguised as an old person
  in a cheap hotel
goes out to ask for carfare.
But I never seem to catch sight of him.
If I did, what would I ask him for?
He has already experienced what is missing in my life.
Kabir says: I belong to this old person.
      Now let the events about to come, come!

Kabir; India, 1450–1518

GUIDE THIS LITTLE BOAT

Guide this little boat
over the waters,
what can I give you for fare?
Our mutable world holds nothing but grief,
bear me away from it.
Eight bonds of karma
have gripped me—
the whole of creation
swirls through eight million wombs,
through eight million birth-forms we flicker.
Mira cries: Dark One—
take this little boat to the far shore,
put an end to coming
and going.

Mirabai; India, 1498–1550,
translated by Andrew Schelling

GOD'S AID

God to enfold me,
   God to surround me,
God in my speaking,
   God in my thinking.

God in my sleeping,
   God in my waking,
God in my watching,
   God in my hoping.

God in my life,
   God in my lips,
God in my soul,
   God in my heart.

God in my sufficing,
   God in my slumber,
God in mine ever-living soul,
   God in mine eternity.

*Celtic oral tradition; collected in
Scotland, nineteenth century*

THOUGH I BE OLD

Thou I be old,
clasp me one night to thy breast,
and I,
when the dawn shall come to awaken me,
with the flush of youth on my cheek
from thy bosom
will rise.

The Divan of Hafiz; medieval Islamic tradition,
c. 1300–1388

IF I HAVE DONE WRONG

If I have done wrong in thought, word, or deed, may Indra,
Varuna, Brhaspati, and Savitr purify me again and again!
Free from my sins, I shall be liberated, freed from guilt, with-
out spot or stain!

Krishna Yajur Veda, Mahānārāyaṇa Upanishad, *132–133; India,
ancient oral tradition, B.C.E., translated by Raimond Panikkar*

WITHOUT GOING OUT OF YOUR DOOR

Without going out of your door
You can know all things on earth.
Without looking out of your window
You can know the ways of the Tao.

For the farther one travels
The less one knows.

The sage therefore
Arrives without leaving,
Sees all without looking,
Does all without doing.

From the Tao Te Ching, *Lao-tzu; China,*
c. 604–531 B.C.E.

In the Evening of the Day

Abide with us, Lord, for it is toward evening and the day is far spent; abide with us and with the whole people of God. Abide with us in the evening of the day, in the evening of life, in the evening of the world. Abide with us and with all your faithful ones, O Lord, in time and eternity.

Anonymous Lutheran prayer; traditional

In Your Midst

I, God, am in your midst.
Whoever knows me can never fall,
Not in the heights,
Nor in the depths,
Nor in the breadths,
For I am love,
Which the vast expanses of evil
Can never still.

Hildegard of Bingen; Germany, 1098–1179

Righteousness

A man is not old and venerable because gray hairs are on his head. If a man is old only in years, then he is indeed old in vain.

But a man is a venerable "elder" if he is in truth free from sin, and if in him there is truth and righteousness, nonviolence, moderation, and self-control.

Not by mere words and appearance can a man be a man of honor, if envy, greed, and deceit are in him. But he in whom these three sins are uprooted and who is wise and has love, is he in truth a man of honor.

The Dhammapada, *260–263; Southeast Asia,*
compiled c. third century B.C.E.

Like Fire

It is God's will to be given completely to us. In the same way, when fire seeks to draw the wood into itself, and to draw itself into the wood again, it finds the wood unlike itself. But all this takes time. First of all, the fire heats the wood, then it smokes and crackles, being unlike the wood, and the hotter the wood becomes, the more still and quiet it grows. The more the wood is like the fire, the more peaceful it is until it turns completely into the fire. If the fire is to press the wood into itself, all unlikeness must be at an end.

Meister Eckhart; Germany, c. 1260–1327,
translated by Matthew Fox

The Lord Is at Hand

Have no anxiety at all,
But in everything,
By prayer and petition,
With thanksgiving,
Let your requests be known to God.
Then the peace of God that
Surpasses all understanding
Will fill your heart and
Your mind
In Christ Jesus.

Philippians 4:6–7

DEATH

The impassioned flood of feelings and images and words that pour forth from the soul in the face of death—one's own, a beloved's, a stranger's—finds expression in prayers all over the world that surpass the finest poetry or prose. Anguish, denial, desperation, despair, blend with longing for an afterlife, for resurrection of the body or soul, for reincarnation, for peaceful release into eternity. Prayers about death convey vividly, frankly, relentlessly, the searing pain involved in the ending of a human life—and transport the experience to the level of immortality.

A breathtaking prayer from the Celtic tradition, "The Lullaby of the Snow," records a legendary story about death in its most cruel role. A young mother is dying, and the small baby she holds in her arms is dying in an unbearable night of agony. Trapped by a massacre in wartime, the mother and child are lost in the snow, alone, dying from the cold and starvation. In the despair of helplessness and hopelessness, the mother addresses the void, and then her child, who is perhaps already dead:

> *Cold, cold this night is my bed,*
> *Cold, cold this night is my child,*

> *Lasting, lasting this night thy sleep*
> *I in my shroud and thou in mine arm.*

As the shadow of death falls more heavily over mother and child, despondence reaches the breaking point, overwhelming and merciless, but no help comes:

> *Though loud my cry my plaint is idle,*
> *Though sore my struggle no friend shares it . . .*
> *Thine eye is closed, thy sleep is heavy,*
> *Thy mouth to my breast, but thou seekest no milk*
> *My croon of love thou shalt never know,*
> *My plaint of love thou shalt never tell.*

Yet even in the midst of such powerless grief, such hopeless anguish, the grace and miracle of faith take place at the center of her soul, and, surrendering, she turns in prayer to the only possible source of solace, the Crucified God:

> *May the angels of God make smooth the road,*
> *May the angels of God be calling us home.*

The tragedy ends, as all tragedy ultimately ends, in Divine embrace, in the arms of God, where grief melts away like snow in spring, and Absolute Love always vanquishes. For in the spiritual life, there is no such thing as death: death is overcome by Eternal Life. Because of the lifelong stream of miracles and mysteries that play out like a holy symphony in the soul, most people on earth believe, like the young woman in the Celtic prayer, that neither time nor space can ever separate those who love.

A triumphal echo of this great victory over grief resounds in Saint Paul's exultant words "O, death, where is thy sting?" (I Corinthians 15:55.) The truth is — as all the world's scriptures affirm — that for people who pray, death itself dies, swallowed up in the holy, imperishable Light of Eternity.

THE LULLABY OF THE SNOW

Cold, cold this night is my bed,
Cold, cold this night is my child,
Lasting, lasting this night thy sleep,
I in my shroud and thou in mine arm.

Over me creeps the shadow of death,
The warm pulse of my love will not stir,
The wind of the heights thy sleep-lulling,
The close-clinging snow of the peaks thy mantle.

Over thee creeps the hue of death,
White angels are floating in the air,
The Son of grace each season guards thee,
The Son of my God keeps the watch with me.

Though loud my cry, my plaint is idle,
Though sore my struggle, no friend shares it;
Thy body-shirt is the snow of the peaks,
Thy death-bed the fen of the valleys.

Thine eye is closed, thy sleep is heavy,
Thy mouth to my breast, but thou seekest no milk;

My croon of love thou shalt never know,
My plaint of love thou shalt never tell.

A cold arm-burden my love on my bosom,
A frozen arm-burden without life or breath;
May the angels of God make smooth the road,
May the angels of God be calling us home.

A hard frost no thaw shall subdue,
The frost of the grave which no spring shall
    make green,
A lasting sleep which morn shall not break,
The death-slumber of mother and child.

Heavenly light directs my feet,
The music of the skies gives peace to my
    soul,
Alone I am under the wing of the Rock,
Angels of God calling me home.

Cold, cold, cold is my child,
Cold, cold is the mother who watches thee,
Sad, sad, sad is my plaint,
As the tinge of death creeps over me.

O Cross of the heavens, sign my soul
O Mother of breastlings, shield my child,
O Son of tears whom a mother nurtured,
Show Thy tenderness in death to the needy.

Celtic oral tradition; collected in Scotland,
nineteenth century

THE HOUR IS NOW COME

O just Creator, ever to be praised, the time is come in which You have ordained that Your servant should be tested. And it is rightly ordained that if I now must suffer, I should suffer for You. The hour is now come that You have known from the beginning, when Your servant should be outwardly set at nothing and inwardly live to You. You have let me become little in the sight of the world, broken with pain and sickness, so that I afterward might rise with You into a new light and be illuminated and made happy in the kingdom of eternity. O Holy God, You have ordained it to be so, and so it is done.

Thomas à Kempis; Germany, 1380–1471

FAREWELL, MY YOUNGER BROTHER

Farewell, my younger brother.
From the highest places
The Gods have come for me.
You will never see me again.
But when the showers pass over you,
And the thunder sounds,
You will pray:
"There is the voice of my elder brother."
And when the harvests ripen,
And you hear the voices
of all the small beautiful birds,
And the grasshoppers chirp,
You will pray:
"There is the voice of my elder brother;
There is the trail of his soul."

Native America; adapted from Navajo oral
tradition

THE LAST WORDS OF TERESA OF ÁVILA

My Lord, it is time to move on.
Well then, may Your will be done.
O my Lord and my Spouse,
the hour that I have longed for has come.
It is time for us to meet one another.

Teresa of Ávila; Spain, 1515–1582

AT DEATH'S DOOR

Lord, please fill my heart with love for your lotus feet, and burn out the seed of every selfish desire and sense craving in my mind.

Grant that I be born in a deeply spiritual family so that my heart may be brimming with devotion for you from the earliest days of my childhood.

Please grant that I may become a humble instrument in your hands to awaken love and devotion for your lotus feet in all human hearts.

Om, shanti, shanti, shanti.

Eknath Easwaran; India, twentieth century

I Am Ready for My Journey

I have got my leave. Bid me farewell, my brothers! I bow to you all and take my departure.

Here I give back the keys of my door—and I give up all claims to my house. I only ask for last kind words from you.

We were neighbors for long, but I received more than I could give. Now the day has dawned and the lamp that lit my dark corner is out. A summons has come and I am ready for my journey.

Rabindranath Tagore; India, 1861–1941

Funeral Chant

O great Nzambi, what thou has made is good, but thou has brought a great sorrow to us with death. Thou shouldst have planned in some way that we would not be subject to death. O Nzambi, we are afflicted with great sadness.

Congo; oral tradition

THE DEATH DIRGE

Thou goest home this night to thy home of winter,
To thy home of autumn, of spring, and of summer;
Thou goest home this night to thy perpetual home,
To thine eternal bed, to thine eternal slumber.

Sleep thou, sleep, and away with thy sorrow,
Sleep thou, sleep, and away with thy sorrow,
Sleep thou, sleep, and away with thy sorrow;
Sleep thou beloved, in the Rock of the fold.

Sleep this night in the breast of thy Mother,
Sleep, thou beloved, while she herself soothes thee;
Sleep thou this night on the Virgin's arm,
Sleep, thou beloved, while she herself kisses thee.

The great sleep of Jesus, the surpassing sleep of Jesus,
The sleep of Jesus' wound, the sleep of Jesus' grief,
The young sleep of Jesus, the restoring sleep of Jesus,
The sleep of the kiss of Jesus of peace and of glory.

The sleep of the seven lights be thine, beloved,
The sleep of the seven joys be thine, beloved,

The sleep of the seven slumbers be thine, beloved,
On the arms of the Jesus of blessings, the Christ of grace.

The shade of death lies upon thy face, beloved,
But the Jesus of grace has His hand round about thee;
    In nearness to the Trinity farewell to thy pains,
Christ stands before thee and peace is in His mind.

The shade of death lies upon thy face, beloved,
But the Jesus of grace has His hand round about thee;
    In nearness to the Trinity farewell to thy pains,
Christ stands before thee and peace is in His mind.

Sleep, O sleep in the calm of all calm,
Sleep, O sleep in the guidance of guidance,
Sleep, O sleep in the love of all loves;
    Sleep, O beloved, in the Lord of life,
    Sleep, O beloved, in the God of life!

Celtic oral tradition; collected in Scotland,
nineteenth century

PILGRIMAGE TO OKINAWA AND KYOTO

I owe my being to untold ancestors.
Some ancestors I have chosen;
others ushered me into this life.
On this sacred journey,
I will meet other ancestors.

My adopted ancestors,
Dharma masters, past and present,
inspire compassionate deeds.
Their aspiration and mine:
Relieve all beings of suffering.

Sakyamuni's cosmic vision:
One is all; all is one,
illumines life and its link with the universe.
We—humanity, the world, all beings—
rise and fall together.

My ancestral spirits, always nearby,
course through and reside in my heart.
What I am and will be,

the fruit of their collective being,
is mirrored in me.

In front of the memorial tablets
they welcome me; I speak with them.
The past is present, the future now.
I belong; my daughter belongs.
I celebrate this mystery with joy and awe.

I am not alone,
nor am I here for myself alone.
I am both heir and ancestor
indebted to all, responsible for all
ancestors of the past, present, and future.

Ronald Y. Nakasone; United States, twentieth century

DEATH LAMENT OF THE TARTARS OF ABAKAN [A PRAYER RECITED AT THE DEATH OF A CHILD]

Why did you give me flocks and herds to cover the
   steppes?
Instead of covering the steppes with herds
You could have given me children.
Though my house is filled, why did you give it, O my God?
Instead of heaping my house with goods,
Why did you not give me a child?

Attributed to the Tartar Prince of the Sagai and his wife, Agylanko;
Khakass Autonomous Region of Russia, oral tradition

PRAYER AT THE TIME OF DEATH

The face of Truth is covered over by a golden vessel. Uncover it, O Lord, that I who love the truth may see it. O Lord, Sole Seer, Controller, Sun, Son of the Father of beings, shine forth, concentrate Your splendor that I may behold Your most glorious form. He who is yonder—the Man yonder—I myself am he! Go, my breath, to the immortal breath. Then may this body end in ashes. Remember, O my mind, the deeds of the past. Remember the deeds, remember the deeds! O Lord, lead us along the right path to prosperity. O God, who knows all our deeds, take from us deceitful sin. To You, then, we shall offer our prayers.

Śukla Yajur Veda, Īśa Upanishad *VII, 59, 10;*
India, c. 4000 B.C.E.,
translated by Raimond Panikkar

In Desperation of Bereavement

My husband, you have abandoned me.
My master is gone and will never return.
I am lost.
I have no hope.
For you used to fetch water and collect firewood for me.
You used to clothe and feed me with good things.
Why have you done thus to me?
Where shall I go?

Anonymous; Uganda, second millennium C.E.

ONLY A LITTLE WHILE HERE

I, Nezahualcoyotl, ask this:
Is it true one really lives on the earth?
Not forever on earth,
only a little while here.
Though it be jade it falls apart,
though it be gold it wears away,
though it be quetzal plumage it is torn asunder.
Not forever on earth,
only a little while here.

Attributed to Nezahualcoyotl; Mexico, 1402–1472,
translated by Miguel Leon-Portilla

DEATH LAMENT

Although thou hast died,
   Love, thou hadst not needed to die;
   Still uam, still am.

Thy little kebbocks of cheese
   Had been placed on the withe;
   Still uam, still am.

Thy little kegs of butter
   Had been smoothed by thy hand;
   Still uam, still am.

And thy little chests of meal
   Had been pressed by thy foot.
   Still uam, still am.

Where shall we go to make our plaint
   When we are hungry on the round?
   Still uam, still am.

Where shall we go to warm ourselves
   When we are chilled with cold?
   Still uam, still am.

Where shall we go for shelter
　　since thy hearth is now dead?
　　Still uam, still am.

Whom shall we resort to and visit
　　Since thy house, love, is cold?
　　Still uam, still am.

Although thou hast died,
　　It was not thy wont to be gloomy;
　　Still uam, still am.

Well mightest thou have stayed
　　To give crowdy to folk.
　　Still uam, still am.

But, O gentle loved Mary,
　　Be thou kind to my love.
　　Still uam, still am.

Celtic oral tradition; collected in Scotland,
nineteenth century

REQUIEM

And so you died as women used to die, at home, in your own warm bedroom, the old-fashioned death of women in labor, who try to close themselves again but can't, because that ancient darkness which they have also given birth to returns for them, thrusts its way in, and enters.

Once, ritual lament would have been chanted; women would have been paid to beat their breasts and howl for you all night, when all is silent. Where can we find such customs now? So many have long since disappeared or have been disowned. That's what you had come for: to retrieve the lament that we omitted. Can you hear me? I would like to fling my voice out like a cloth over the fragments of your death, and keep pulling at it until it is torn to pieces, and all my words would have to walk around shivering, in the tatters of that voice; if lament were enough.

Rainer Maria Rilke; Germany, 1875–1926,
translated by Stephen Mitchell

Lament of the Flutes for Tammuz

When he is no more, a lament rises:
"O my loved one."
When he is no more, her lament rises:
"O my loved one."
When he is no more, her lament rises:
"O my enchanter!"
When he is no more, her lament rises:
Under the silvery cedar, vast-limbed and shady,
At Eanna, over mountains and dales, her lament rises.
The lament says that a home is rising to weep with her.
No longer does the grass have roots;
No longer does the grain have heads;
No longer is there joy in the dwelling.
She is a tired woman, a maiden withered too soon.
The river weeps for the willow that no longer grows;
Fields weep for the herbs and grains that now grow not;
Swamps weep for the lake and the fish that have gone;
Forests weep for the glades that are parched;

Hills and plains weep for the cypress;
The vineyard weeps for the dead vine;
Pastures weep for the missing flowers;
The Palace weeps for the life that is no more.

Mesopotamia; ancient oral tradition

THE KADDISH

Let us magnify and let us sanctify the great name of God in the world which He created according to His will. May His kingdom come in your lifetime, and in your days, and in the lifetime of the family of Israel—quickly and speedily may it come. Amen.

May the greatest of His being be blessed from eternity to eternity.

Let us bless and let us extol, let us tell aloud and let us raise aloft, let us set on high and let us honor, let us exalt and let us praise the Holy One—blessed be He!—though He is far beyond any blessing or song, any honor or any consolation that can be spoken of in this world. Amen.

May great peace from heaven and the gift of life be granted to us and to all the family of Israel. Amen.

May He who makes peace in the highest bring this peace upon us and upon all Israel. Amen.

Traditional Jewish prayer

A Meditation on Death

Yea, O my God, it is thou that must raise up this faint and drooping heart of mine. Thou only canst rid me of this weak and cowardly distrust. Thou that sendest forth my soul canst prepare it for thyself; thou only canst make thy messenger welcome to me. O that I could but see thy face through death! O that I could see death not as it was but as thou hast made it. O that I could heartily pledge thee, my savior, in this cup, that so I might drink new wine with thee in thy father's kingdom.

But alas, O my God, nature is strong and weak in me at once. I cannot wish to welcome death as it is worthy; when I look for most courage, I find most temptations. I see and confess that when I am myself, thou hast no such coward as I. Let me alone and I shall shame that name of thine which I have professed. Every secure worldling shall laugh at my feebleness . . . O God, let it be no shame for thy servant to take up that complaint which thou mads't of thy better attendants, "The spirit is willing, but the flesh is weak."

O thou God of spirits that hast coupled these two together, unite them in a desire of their dissolution. Weaken this flesh to receive, and encourage this spirit either to desire or to contemn death. And now as I grow nearer to my home, let me increase in the sense of my joys. I am thine. Save me, O Lord.

Joseph Hall; England, 1574–1656

At the Time of Death of a Loved One

O Lord, let us be imbued with sacred truths during this soul's great passage to great realms. Pain and pleasure — both are unreal. The Soul, the Atman, the Divine Self within, is ever immersed in Divine love. You exist as pure knowledge itself, so deluding joy and grief cannot touch You any more than fire can melt a stone.

[MOURNERS:] Do not harbor thoughts of past actions, but with all the power at your command let your inner being yearn and draw near to the gracious presence of your holy and ever-gracious God and Spiritual Guru. Like the water welling up from a spring, carry on your heartfelt praise and worship. In sweet harmony live on, be free of resolve and doubt, and remain calm in perfect poise and serenity.

Relish the gift, the nectar of spiritual consciousness that endows you with insight and detachment. Let the vision of harmonious Reality dawn, when the unknown Truth of God and the known untruth of life shall merge in the bliss of liberation.

Maha Yogi Siva Yogaswami; Sri Lanka, 1872–1964

A Bahá'í Prayer for the Deceased

O my Lord,
Purify them from trespasses,
dispel their sorrows,
and change their darkness into light.
Cause them to enter the garden of happiness,
cleanse them with the most pure water,
and grant them to behold Thy splendors
on the loftiest mount.

'Abdu'l-Bahá; Iran, 1844–1921

I Am the Resurrection and the Life

I am the resurrection and the life; he that believeth in me, though he were dead, yet shall he live, and whosoever liveth and believeth in me shall never die.

The eternal God is thy refuge, and underneath are the everlasting arms.

The Lord is my light and my salvation; whom shall I fear? The Lord is the strength of my life; of whom shall I be afraid?

The righteous live forever, and the care of them is with the most High; with his right hand he shall cover them, and with his arm shall he shield them.

For we know that if our earthly house of this tabernacle were dissolved, we have a building of God, a house not made with hands, eternal in the heavens.

From the Christian Order for the Burial of the Dead; traditional

ZUÑI DEATH CRY

My God! My God!
  Why hast Thou abandoned me?

  Hi-ihiya, naiho-o
  It is finished,
  In beauty, it is finished.
    Nai-ho-o.

  Zuñi oral tradition; Native America

NUNC DIMITTIS

Lord, now lettest Thou Thy servant depart in peace,
according to Thy word:
For mine eyes have seen Thy salvation,
Which Thou hast prepared before the face of all people;
A light to lighten the Gentiles,
and the glory of Thy people Israel.

Luke 2:29–32

I Am Going Home with Thee

I am going home with thee
   To thy home! to thy home!
I am going home with thee
   To thy home of winter.

I am going home with thee
   To thy home! to thy home!
I am going home with thee
   To thy home of autumn, of spring and of summer.

I am going home with thee,
   Thou child of my love,
To thine eternal bed,
   To thy perpetual sleep.

I am going home with thee,
   Thou child of my love,
To the dear Son of blessing,
   To the Father of grace.

Celtic oral tradition; collected in Scotland,
nineteenth century

LET THE ETERNAL DAWN BREAK

Receive into Paradise, O Lord,
all those who will sleep tonight
and not awaken again.

Let the eternal dawn break for them
through the Lord our God
now and forevermore.

Amen.

Traditional Christian prayer

FREE FROM ALL SORROWS

The traveler has reached the end of the journey! In the freedom of the Infinite he is free from all sorrows; the fetters that bound him are thrown away, and the burning fever of life is no more.

The Dhammapada, *90; Southeast Asia, compiled c. third century*
B.C.E.

CONCLUDING PRAYER

MAY OUR PRAYERS BE PLEASING

May You, O Lord,
find the fragrance of our prayers pleasing,
and through the perfume of Your incense,
may Your creatures be reconciled to You,
for the sake of Your mercy,
now and forever and until the world's end.

*From the Eastern Christian Liturgy; Syria, fourth
or fifth century*

AFTERWORD

oday, as the world grows smaller and more dangerous, the life of prayer offers perhaps the only hope there is of weaving the tattered threads of the human fabric into the sacred tapestry it was meant to be. Prayer has the power to draw warring people together into community, to negate the differences doctrines create, to express a uniquely human experience of beauty, suffering, longing, and love. As Karl Rahner once wrote:

> In the deep interior quiet (of prayer), the finer things in life take place. The huge negative forces Freud defined are stilled, and in the deep pool of inner humility, music is heard, love is felt, beauty experienced.

It is my hope that this book will inspire prayer, and that prayer will ennoble life, dignify the human condition, and reveal the great integrity inherent in the human soul.

ACKNOWLEDGMENTS

To the American Bible Society, New York: for Psalms 121 and 139, and Luke 2:29–32, from *The Holy Bible*, Authorized, 1877.

To Astor-Honor: for prayers from *The Prayers of Man*, by Alfonso M. DiNola, © 1961, reprinted by permission of Astor-Honor, Division of Beauty Fashion, New York, NY 10036.

To Ballantine Books: for a prayer from *American Indian Poetry*, by George Cronyn, editor. Copyright © 1918, 1934, renewed 1962 by George Cronyn. Reprinted by permission of Ballantine Books, a Division of Random House, Inc.

To Beacon Press: for two poems from *The Kabir Book*, by Robert Bly. Copyright © 1971, 1977 by Robert Bly. Reprinted by permission of Beacon Press, Boston, MA.

To Bear and Co.: for two meditations from *Meditations with Meister Eckhart*, by Matthew Fox. Copyright 1983, Bear and Co., Inc., P.O. Box 2860, Santa Fe, NM 87504.

To Columbia University Press: for eight lines from *Cold Mountain*, by Burton Watson. Copyright © 1970 by Columbia University Press. Reprinted with the permission of the publisher.

To Darton, Longman, and Todd, Ltd., and Doubleday and Company, Inc., New York, NY: for Ephesians 3:16–21, from

The Jerusalem Bible, Alexander Jones, editor, copyright © 1966, 1967, 1968.

To Frog, Ltd.: for a poem from *The Way of Passion: A Celebration of Rumi*, by Andrew Harvey (Berkeley, CA: Frog. Ltd., 1994). Used by permission.

To Gaba Publications: for permission to reprint prayers in "Spearhead" #89, granted by Gaba Publications, Eldoret, Kenya.

To Ghetto Fighter's House, Israel: for "Passover, Bergen-Belsen, 1944," letter dated June 13, 1959, to P. Goodman from Zvi Shener, Ghetto Fighter's House, in Memory of Yitzhak Katznelson, Israel. By permission of the Ghetto Fighter's House.

To HarperCollins: for number 8 from *Tao Te Ching*. Translation copyright © 1988 by Stephen Mitchell. Reprinted by permission of HarperCollins Publishers, Inc., New York, NY. And for lines from *Buddhist Texts Through the Ages*, by Edward Conze, editor, copyright © 1964.

To *Intermountain Catholic:* for "A Sixteen-Year-Old Gangster's Prayer," *Intermountain Catholic*, Vol. 5, No. 22, June 17, 1994.

To Alfred A. Knopf, Inc.: for "On Birth" and "On Marriage" from *The Prophet* by Kahlil Gibran, © 1923 by Kahlil

Gibran and renewed 1951 by Administrators C.T.A. of Kahlil Gibran Estate and Mary G. Gibran. Reprinted by permission of Alfred A. Knopf, Inc.

To Dr. Miguel Leon-Portilla of the Instituto de Investigaciones Historicas, Universidád Nacionál Autónoma de México: for permission to reprint a translation from Nezahualcoyotl.

To the National Spiritual Assembly of the Bahá'ís of the United States: for prayers from *Bahá'í Prayers*, copyright 1954, © 1982, 1985, 1991 by the National Spiritual Assembly of the Bahá'ís of the United States. *Prayers and Meditations*, copyright © 1938 by the National Spiritual Assembly of the Bahá'ís of the United States. *Selections from the Writings of the Bab*, copyright © 1976 by the Universal House of Justice. And *The Seven Valleys and the Four Valleys*, copyright © 1945, 1952, 1973, 1975, 1978 by the National Spiritual Assembly of the Bahá'ís of the United States.

To *New Menorah*, the journal of ALEPH, Aliance for Jewish Renewal, 7318 Germantown Avenue, Philadelphia, PA 19119: for permission to reprint "Haftarah for a Covenant of Comforting," copyright © 1994 by Arthur Waskow.

To Oxford University Press: for Prayer No. 961 in the *Oxford Book of Prayers*, from Soyen Shaku. Reprinted from *Zen*

To the Smithsonian Institution, Washington, D.C., U.S. Bureau of American Ethnology: for Native American prayers from *Bulletins* 1–163, 1888–1956.

To SPCK, Holy Trinity Church, Marylebone Road, London, England: for permission to reprint prayers from *The Prayers of African Religion*, by J. S. Mbiti.

To Through the Flower, Albuquerque, NM 87105: for permission to reprint Judy Chicago's poem "Merger."

To Westminster Synagogue, London, England: for permission to reprint prayers from *Daily and Sabbath Prayer Book*, © 1992.

INDEX OF TITLES

An author of both inspirational and scholarly works, a religious researcher and former college teacher, Mary Ford-Grabowsky is editor of *Fellowship in Prayer* in Princeton, New Jersey. She has a doctorate in theology and spirituality from Princeton Theological Seminary, as well as a master of divinity degree, and translates prayers from French, German, Spanish, Italian, and Latin into English. For over nine years, she has conducted research on prayer in Europe, Latin America, and the United States. She serves on the board of trustees of several organizations, among them Friends of Creation Spirituality, Inc., founded by Matthew Fox. She is married and has a daughter at Stanford Medical School.